GW00832006

IBIZA
FORMENTERA

Authors:
Roland Mischke
Berthold Schwarz

An Up-to-date travel guide
with 56 color photos
and 7 maps

NELLES

IMPRINT / LEGEND

Dear Reader: Being up to date is the main goal of the Nelles series. Our correspondents help keep us abreast of the latest developments in the travel scene while our cartographers see to it that maps are also kept completely current. However, as the travel world is constantly changing we cannot guarantee that all the information contained in our books is always valid. Should you come across a discrepancy please contact us at: Nelles Verlag, Schleissheimer Str. 371 b, 80935 Munich, Germany, tel. (089) 3571940, fax (089) 35719430, e-mail: Nelles.Verlag@t-online.de, Internet: www.Nelles-Verlag.de

Note: Distances, measurements and temperatures used in this guide are metric. For conversion information, please see the *Travel Information* section of this book.

LEGEND

★★	Main Attraction *(on map)*	**Sant Joan***(Town)*	Places Highlighted in Yellow Appear in Text	Throughway
★★	*(in text)*	*Es Cavallet (Sight)*		Principal Highway
★	Worth Seeing *(on map)*	✈	International airport	Main Road
★	*(in text)*			Provincial Road
❽	Orientation Number in Text and on Map	**Puig Gros** 403	Mountain peak (altitude in meters)	Secondary Road
▪	Public or Significant Building	⚑ 13 ⚑	Distance in kilometers	Track, Path
■ ●	Hotel, Restaurant	☀	Beach	Pedestrian Zone/ Promenade
▨	Market	⊟	Bus station	Ferry
ℹ	Touristinformation	△	Campsite	⑤⑤⑤ Luxury Hotel Category
✝ ⛪	Church	▮ ⸾	Tower, Lighthouse	⑤⑤ Moderate Hotel Category
※ ⛳	View Point, Golf Course	∴ ∩	Ancient site, Cave	⑤ Budget Hotel Category *(for price information see "Accomodation" in Guidelines section)*

IBIZA – FORMENTERA
© Nelles Verlag GmbH, 80935 Munich
  All rights reserved

First Edition 2001
ISBN 3-88618-768-3 (Nelles Travel Pack)
ISBN 3-88618-864-7 (Nelles Pocket)
Printed in Slovenia

Publisher:	Günter Nelles	**Lithography:**	Priegnitz, München
Managing Editor:	Berthold Schwarz	**Cartography:**	Nelles Verlag GmbH, München
Photo Editor:	K. Bärmann-Thümmel		
English Edition Translator: Kerstin Borch		**Printed by:**	Gorenjski Tisk

No part of this book, not even excerpts, may be reproduced in any form without the express written permission of Nelles Verlag
- S01 -

TABLE OF CONTENTS

TRAVEL INFORMATION

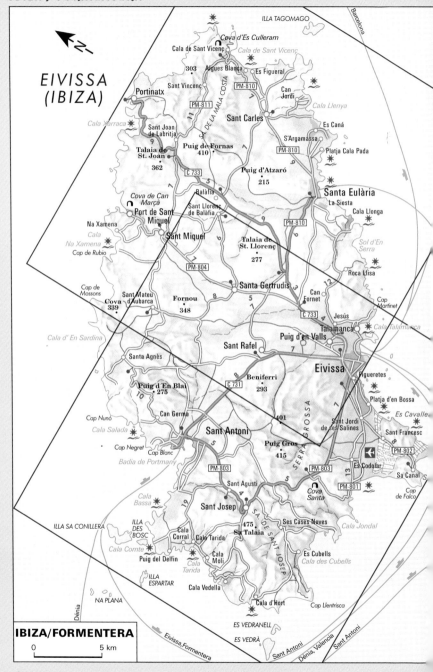

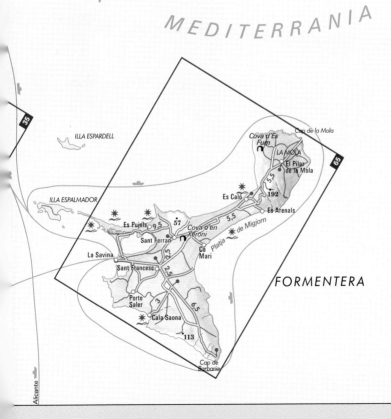

Prehistory

Ca. 2000 B.C. The megalithic dolmen tomb of Ca na Costa is the earliest documented settlement on the *Pitiusas* (Ibiza and Formentera).

Ca. 700 B.C. Carthaginians drop anchor near Sa Caleta in Ibiza's southwest and prepare to settle permanently due to the island's strategic location.

The Carthaginians on Ibiza

654 B.C. The Carthaginians found the town of *Ibosim* – modern-day Eivissa – in honor of their god, Bes (Ibosim = "Island of Bes"); the salt trade brings wealth to the island.

5th century B.C. The Carthaginians systematically inhabit the island's interior and cultivate the land.

247 B.C. Hannibal, the legendary general of Carthage, is supposedly born on an islet off Ibiza's coast.

218-201 B.C. The Carthaginians are defeated by the Romans in the Second Punic War, but the Punic culture continues to influence the Pitiusas.

Arrival of the Romans

123 B.C. The Romans conquer and colonize the Balearic Islands; Ibosim is renamed Ebusus.

70 A.D. The islands are incorporated into the Roman Empire, resulting in an economic upswing.

380 A.D. Christianity becomes the Roman state religion and the official faith of the Pitiusas.

426 A.D. The Vandals conquer the Pitiusas.

5th/6th centuries Following constant attacks by Germanic tribes (Visigoths and Ostrogoths) the Roman Empire is divided up into the Western Roman and Eastern Roman (Byzantine) Empire. In 535 the islands are handed over to Byzantium (Eastern Roman Empire), but only nominally.

8th/9th centuries For two centuries the Pitiusas are tossed from one occupant to the next. Invaders include the Arabs, Franks and Normans. But for now not one of these invaders succeeds in permanently conquering the island.

Under the Banner of Islam

902 Moors conquer Ibiza under the leadership of the Calif of Cordoba and rename the island's capital Medina Iabissa. They spread the Islamic faith and introduce irrigation techniques and agricultural terracing.

After 1076 Muslim pirates establish a base on the Balearics and operate from there.

1114 Although Catalans and Pisans occupy Mallorca for 2 years the Pitiusas remain a Moorish pirate stronghold.

Catalan Reconquista

1235 In the wake of the "reconquista" the Catalan knights take the islands and expel the Muslims. All the towns are renamed after Christian saints and Catalan becomes the official language.

The Carthaginians imported their own goddess – Tanit.

1276 The kingdom of Mallorca, which includes Ibiza and Formentera, is founded.

1299 Thanks to the establishment of the "Universidad" the Balearics are granted their own independent administration.

1349 James III of Mallorca is killed in battle with Spanish troops from the mainland; the Balearic kingdom falls to the King of Aragón and is put under a great deal of pressure through tax burdens; economic crisis ensues on the Pitiusas.

The Pitiusas under Spanish Rule

15th/16th century A united Spain – which became a major world power after the discovery of America – develops on the mainland after 1486, but Ibiza and Formentera remain commercially neglected. Poverty is rife among the islanders. Piracy drives out many of Ibiza's inhabitants and Formentera is depopulated completely.

1550 Charles V orders fortification of the coasts and towns: from 1554 on Eivissa has a town wall; several defense towers are erected around the coast.

The Portal de Ses Taules is the main gateway to Eivissa's upper town, a UNESCO site.

17th-19th century With the permission of the Spanish king Ibizan corsairs voyage out on the Mediterranean on a pillaging spree.

1701 During the Spanish War of Succession the Pitiusans side with the Habsburgs, but they are both defeated by the Castilians whose soldiers occupy the islands and then give them to the Bourbons.

1717 The salinas are exploited by the Catalan government on the island; the Pitiusas are struck by a wave of poverty.

1726 Formentera is resettled.

1782 Eivissa is awarded its own administration and becomes an episcopal seat.

1867 Habsburg archduke Ludwig Salvator is the first "tourist" to visit the Pitiusas; he writes several volumes about the island, its people and customs.

1878 Steamboats operate regularly between Ibiza and Barcelona.

The 20th Century

From 1930 Europe's artists discover the Pitiusas, including the writers Walter Benjamin and Raoul Hausmann. The first hotels on Ibiza are opened in 1933.

1936-1939 Franco's clerical-fascist troops invade Ibiza during the Spanish Civil War; Formentera becomes a prison island. The Catalan language is forbidden under Franco.

1958 The period of mass tourism commences with the opening of Eivissa's airport and the arrival of the first charter airline.

From 1968 The global hippie movement "conquers" both islands.

1983 The Balearic Islands are declared an autonomous region and Catalan is reinstated as the official language.

1986 Spain joins the European Union, tourism on the Balearics is promoted; the building of sprawling hotel complexes on Formentera is halted just in time.

From 1990 Mass tourism suffers a crisis, the industry is forced to sit back and re-evaluate. In the mid-90s the Pitiusas emerge from the crisis stronger than before thanks to a massive offensive accompanied by an image campaign under the motto "Ibiza is different."

1999 A new Balearic government – a Social-Democratic and Green coalition contrasting the political trends on the mainland – replaces the Partido Popular, Spain's Civil Conservative Party which was in power for decades. A drastic building stop within 500 meters of the coastal zones and strict environmental laws are enforced. 1.6 million people, including 711,000 Britons, visit the Pitiusas that year.

2000 1.9 million tourists visit Ibiza and Formentera.

2001 The Basque underground organization ETA threatens to bomb tourist destinations on the Balearic Islands.

LAND AND PEOPLE

The two southermost Balearics, Ibiza and Formentera, are also known as *las Islas Pitiusas*. The term was coined by the seafaring Greeks and means "pine-covered islands." Blankets of evergreen aleppo pines thrive here, as well as the cypress-shaped Phoenician juniper. Fruit trees characterize the landscape and yield olives, almonds, figs, oranges, lemons and carob. Fallow land is blanketed by mostly macchia or garigue scrub. Dense underwater prairies of oceanic *posidonia* (seagrass which enriches the seas off Ibiza and Formentera with oxygen) have been declared a UNESCO World Heritage site.

Ibiza, the "White Island," is 541 km² in area, 41 kilometers long and, on average, 20 kilometers wide. By contrast, the island of Formentera is quite tiny, measuring a mere 82 km² in area. Numerous tiny, uninhabited islets are sprinkled in the 3 kilometers of sea between the two – these straits are known by the name of "Es Freus." Geologically speaking all of the islands, including the two large ones, are the summits of a massive underwater range of limestone mountains. Formentera is relatively bare, flat and dry, but is blessed with a very long sand beach; Ibiza, on the other hand, has a more undulating and lush landscape, and apart from its few large beaches is home to mostly small sand bays (*calas*) – in fact, more than 50 of them!

Water temperatures range from 15 °C in April when the holiday season begins to 25 °C in high summer. The crops already start to ripen in the fields in May and are harvested from June on. Some

Preceding pages: The magical rocky islets of Es Vedrà, Es Vedranell and the Torre del Pirata. Left: These days the women of the island only wear their opulent traditional costume to folkloric events (Sant Miguel de Balansat).

farmers still reap their fields with the help of draught horses and in keeping with tradition toss the cereal high into the air so that the wind separates the wheat from the chaff. In early summer the beguiling scent of herbs – above all rosemary and thyme – wafts through the air.

The Ibizan summer is long but never unpleasantly hot; the climate on the Pitiusas is more balanced than on, for example, the Gimnesias (Mallorca, Menorca and Cabrera). Mercury levels rarely rise above 30 degrees and a fresh breeze is usually swept in from the sea.

The tourist season ends in October and from November a cool southwesterly wind embraces the islands. But one can still swim at this time of year in some of the more sheltered areas where the water temperatures remain at a pleasant 21 °C. This out-of-season swimming indulgence is, needless to say, more popular with northern Europeans than locals. October presents an average 8 days of precipitation; this slight dampness in the air is barely comparable to the quantities of water bucketing down in more northerly European regions. "Winter" here implies average daytime temperatures of around 15 °C (approx. 8 °C at night) and only the islanders feel the need for warm coats at this time of year. Average daily hours of sunshine are between five in winter and ten in summer – dream weather by any standards, even better than Mallorca.

Even though Mallorca and Menorca are nearby "Mallorca is like another continent to us," says Jorge Alonso, director of the Ibizan tourist board, "and Europe is like another planet. When we go to the Spanish mainland we say we're going to Europe. A visit to Germany or Britain would be equivalent to a trip to Mars. Naturally, America and Australia are located in entirely different galaxies."

Today the original language of the Pitiusas is being spoken once again: *Eivissenc*, a dialect of Catalan and an independent Romance language like

what really sets them apart is the fact that they are islanders and have spent much of their history experiencing foreigners as a threat: pirates posed a great danger for the coastal regions for over one thousand years; whole villages were wiped out by these seafaring criminals, natives were brutally murdered, families were torn apart, women and children were kidnapped. Although, it must be mentioned that the islanders occasionally topped up their own pocket money by indulging in a little piracy themselves. For the longest time in the history of the Pitiusas life for the islanders was full of hardship and privation as they lived mainly from their agricultural means, which was difficult enough as Formentera only gets about 384 mm of rain annually. Fishing was the second most important source of food.

The natives are rather reserved, but extremely tolerant. Hurrying or pushing is considered bad manners, hasty decisions are frowned upon and they formulate unpleasant but necessary truths in a charmingly decorative, roundabout way. Around 85,000 people live on both islands today, yet only 35,000 of them were actually born here. The rest are Spanish, hailing from the Iberian peninsula, or people from other European countries who were attracted by the sun.

Nowadays the Balearics belong to the wealthiest regions of Spain. Tourists were the first "invaders" to ever bring economic wealth to the island, but at the same time tourism has also resulted in social restructuring on the Pitiusas: from a rural, farming society to a modern one.

Despite the immense changes that have taken place in the lives of the islanders the age-old customs and traditions dating back to Punic, Roman and Arab times have been faithfully preserved. For example the typical flat-roofed farmhouses (*fincas*) consisting of several cubic buildings grouped around one large residential area resemble the architectural style of the North African Berbers.

Mallorcan and Menorcan, was forbidden until Franco's death in 1975 and could only be spoken at home within the family, even though Castilian – Spain's official language – was often not understood by older members of the island population. Today their language is sacred to them: it bridges the generations and protects the populace from foreign infiltration. "Menja fort, caga fort i no tenguis por la mort!" – "eat well, move your bowels well, and you need never fear death!" Since 1991 only Catalan place names and descriptions are considered official on the Balearics and Ibiza's capital has reclaimed its original name, Eivissa.

Although Spanish the Ibicencos are still somehow different – their ancestry includes Phoenician, Roman, Arab, Berber, Jewish and Catalan conquerors. But

Above: Watchtowers such as this one near Punta de sa Torre served to warn and protect the islanders from pirate attacks. Right: Since antiquity salt has been extracted from these salt flats and exported.

Traditional costume is only worn at folk festivals nowadays, where typical oriental-sounding flute, drum and castanet music is played and people sing the old *gaites* songs and dance together. Imitators of the mythical *honderos* (*foners*) – slingshooters who served as soldiers in Hannibal's army and fought against the Romans – are still a feature of sports competitions today. The ancient Greeks named them *Balearides*, hence the name of the archipelago. In 218 B.C. the Carthaginian general crossed the Alps with his elephants, a huge army of soldiers and hundreds of Balearic artillery men armed with slingshots (*bassetja*) with the intention of invading Rome. But the Romans were the victors. They took Ibiza after the fall of Carthage and gained the island's rich salinas which have been a source of wealth for over 2,000 years.

The fact that the island became a holiday mecca in the 20th century can be attributed to the word-of-mouth propaganda spread by the hippies who since the mid-1960s steadily increased their contingent as the pioneers of tourism on the islands. The unsuspecting islanders were surprised by this invasion, but remained tolerant. Which is how an eclectic and colorful mix of eccentric flower children and farmers, shepherds and craftsmen evolved on the island of Formentera and the hinterlands of Ibiza.

The economic backbone of the Pitiusas is package tourism, but it must be said that the "party island" of Ibiza has gone to great efforts recently to upgrade its sangria-guzzling disco image – after all, it also has a lot of historical culture to offer: Eivissa's old town is on the UNESCO list, its museums contain unique finds from the Carthaginian period and its fashion designers, painters and craftsmen are extraordinarily creative. Formentera on the other hand – that little airport-less island with an abundance of rustic charm – traditionally attracts individual travelers and beach tourists seeking peace and nature and the simple things, who prefer to eat breakfast in the mornings instead of shuffling into a daytime discotheque.

EIVISSA
(IBIZA TOWN)

NEW TOWN

LA MARINA

SA PENYA

DALT VILA

MARINA D'ES BOTAFOC

PUIG DES MOLINS

PLATJA D'EN BOSSA

**EIVISSA

History

**Eivissa was founded by the North African Carthaginians around 654 B.C. They worshiped a goddess named Tinnit (which eventually evolved into *Tanit*) – patron saint of their island. They considered her the wife of their main god, Baal, and she represented fertility and death; they even sacrificed their children to her.

The Second Punic War, a veritable bloodbath, took place between 218 and 201 B.C.; the Romans were the victors of the carnage. The defeated Carthaginians were forced to relinquish their bases on *Ibosim* (or Island of Bes, as Ibiza had been named in honor of their god, Bes). The Romans moved in and colonized the Balearics in 123 B.C. and Ibosim was latinized to *Ebusus*. In 70 A.D. a new era began for the Pitiusas: Emperor Vespasian granted Ebusus autonomous minting rights, marking the end of its primitive period. Salt and lead were

Preceding pages: The Platja de Ses Salines (Platja de Migjorn) is one of Ibiza's most beautiful beaches and a "hot spot" for all who wish to see and be seen. Left: A good meal in the old town proves an ideal way to end a perfect day in Eivissa.

mined on the outskirts of modern-day Eivissa, the salinas near Platja de es Cavallet attest to this. The spot where today's cathedral stands was once the site of a Mercury temple built by Emperor Marcus Aurelius in 283.

The town of Eivissa survived many raids and had to stand up to innumerable attacks over the centuries. A colorful array of foreign occupiers settled here, from the Vandals (5th/6th centuries) and Byzantines, Arabs, Franks and Normans (8th century) to the Arab Moors (10th-13th century). The Moorish period was a good time for the city; the *Madina Yabisah* was extended in 902 and was allocated a triple ring of walls and a network of lanes.

As a consequence of the *reconquista* the Spaniards forced the Muslims back toward the African continent after which Eivissa, captured by crusaders in the year 1235, was upgraded in Christian status but was quickly forgotten again by the crown and the archbishops. The city deteriorated and was frequently invaded by pirates who raged through its narrow lanes with barbarous cruelty. It wasn't until the 16th century that Charles V ordered the fortification of Eivissa; the town's new ring of walls would ensure better defense against invasion, pillaging and plundering. In 1652 it was home to

1,000 residents, but in that year half of those lives were abruptly taken by the plague. Felipe V, who ruled Spain from 1717, was responsible for the island's commercial exploitation followed by sheer neglect and before long decline set in once again. Eivissa had never been held in particularly high regard by the Spanish crown and it had only ever represented a strategic base for the military.

In 1782 Pope Pius VI conferred Eivissa's code of law and promoted the city to an episcopal seat. It wasn't until the late 19th century through numerous new constructions, conversions and extensions that Eivissa received it's current architectural appearance. Today 42,000 people proudly call this city their home and the capital's Catalan name, *Eivissa*, has been in official use again since 1991.

Above: Carefully restored Patrician residences from the 19th century line the Passeig Vara de Rey. Right: Ibiza is the birthplace of Ad-lib fashion which is now famous throughout the world.

*THE NEW TOWN AND *LA MARINA

The old harbor quarter of La Marina and the fishing quarter of Sa Penya extend at the foot of the fortified old town and together form the historically-laden lower town, ideal strolling territory.

Pastel-colored Patrician houses from the turn of the 19th/20th centuries line the ****Passeig Vara de Rey ❶** – Eivissa's fashionable main boulevard. This is a privileged, top-class address for retail businesses and gastronomy establishments. The Passeig represents the heart of the city. The **Monument a Vara de Rey** in the center of the promenade honors General Joaquín Vara de Rey i Rubió. This popular Ibicenco, depicted on a pedestal brandishing a sword, fell for Spain in the Cuban War of 1898 when her only remaining colony was lost to the United States of America. The ***Montesol**, the oldest hotel-restaurant in town (established in 1936), stands at the corner of the harbor. Native business people drink their

coffee and *orxata* (almond milk) inside while from the terrace tourists cast an eye over the bustle of the main pedestrian thoroughfare. Around the corner on **Avinguda Ramon y Tur** you'll spot the trendy ★**Mar y Sol** café and a little higher up you'll see the façade of the ★**Teatro Pereira**, a jazz bar with a plush Art Deco interior. 50 meters south of Passeig Vara de Rey the tranquil square **Plaça d'es Parque** with its expansive plane trees is an ideal spot for a coffee break, perhaps in the **Sunset Café**; more often than not you'll be able to watch street artists at work here.

Along **Carrer d'Annibal, Plaça de Sa Font ②** and **Carrer d'Antoni Palau** in the old harbor quarter of ★**La Marina** a sophisticated architectural ensemble presents itself: two and three-storey houses with wrought-iron balconies and enclosed alcoves, all in a rich blaze of color.

By way of **Carrer Josep Verdera** (pedestrian zone) you'll come to the church of **Sant Elm ③**, originally a small fishermens' chapel. Franco's marauding soldiers blasted it to pieces in 1936, but it was magnificently rebuilt after the war. Inside it houses a modern statue of Christ and an old Eivissan crucifix depicting Christ in a red embroidered frock fringed with gold, as he is also depicted in the mystical games of Roman Catholicism where soldiers dice around the frock, as well as a modern statue of Christ just over the altar.

At the **harbor**, near the docks for the ferries to Denia, Barcelona and Mallorca, you'll see an obelisk known as the **Monument al Corsaris ④** which recalls Antonio Riquer Arabí (1773-1846). This Sa Penyan corsair and captain was promoted to the privileged status of folk hero for capturing and sinking enemy vessels. Arabís' most spectacular operation took place in 1806 when he boarded the British frigate vessel *Felicity* close to the harbor and captured her commanding officer, the infamous pirate Miguel Novelli. This monument was donated by Arabí's descendants.

*SA PENYA

The former fishing quarter of ***Sa Penya** is nestled into the slope below the fortress-like upper town. The colorful old buildings mostly accommodate cafés and bars.

Ibiza's fashion industry has chosen the old fishing town – the former seafarers' quarter – as the ideal place for exhibiting its creations. Boutiques can be found in even the most out-of-the-way lanes and they offer everything from high-class fashions to shrill and daringly extravagant pieces. *Ad-lib fashion*, born of the hippie culture at the end of the sixties – *ad libitum* meaning improvisation and spontaneity – boasts its most faithful following here. This fashion style made Ibiza famous throughout the world and its products are still a much-prized commodity on the export market. However, it's far more fitting to acquire the clothes in the original Sa Penyan environment – the place of their creation. Those seeking extravagant leather designs blending Spanish and North African stylistic elements, or beautiful white lace dresses, outrageous shoes, handmade sandals, belts or bags, will certainly strike gold in Sa Penya. *Ad-lib Fashion Week* takes place every June, when Ibizan designers present fashion shows centering around their latest fantastical trends.

Around 650 B.C. the first Ibicencos settled around the location of today's harbor mole and along the narrow ****Carrer de la Virgen** ❺ (*Carrer de Mare Déu*) where everybody meets in the evenings – including the shrillest and most colorful members of the gay scene.

At the end of the mole the small restored defense tower of **Sa Torre** ❻ stands brave against the elements. Narrow lanes lead from Carrer de la Virgen to **Carrer d'Emnig** ❼ just below it which some Ibiza fans, out of habit, still fondly refer to as *Calle Mayor*. You'll find many boutiques, bars and shops here.

The ***Avinguda de Andenes** ❽ and **Passeig des Moll** together comprise the infamous "**circuit**" or "runway" where party-goers like to strut their stuff before setting off for the clubs around midnight.

The Sa Penya quarter sandwiched between the sea and the upper town has retained its original romantic flair. It also reveals a lot about the island's appetite: the old market hall – the ***Mercat Vell** ❾ (specializing in fruit and vegetables), where an almost "Phoenician" trading and haggling atmosphere prevails, is an experience unto itself. It is surrounded by a multitude of small, well-frequented shops and bars on the **Plaça de la Constitució** which are extremely popular, like the **Croissant Show** for example.

**DALT VILA

Dalt Vila, the fortress-like, originally (and until the 13th century) Arab
old town, also known as the upper town,
is characterized by cobblestone lanes. It
was declared a UNESCO world heritage
site in 1999. Dalt Vila is surrounded by a
wall designed by Italian architect
Giovanni Batista Calvi, which took 40
years to build; it was reinforced by six
bulwarks or heavy artillery bases. Charles
I had ordered its building in 1554 and had
to borrow 20,000 ducats from the Bishop
of Valencia in order to properly fortify the
city. Calvi, by then renowned for also
completing splendid works in Barcelona,
Milan and Siena, died in 1561; the remaining work on the wall was carried out
according to his original plans. After ve-
hement Turkish attacks following Calvi's
death the complex was further extended
by Italian architect Jocopo Paleazzo, thus
receiving an additional projection of
walls. Ten hectares were walled in, behind which the local populace would en-
trench themselves whenever danger
loomed. Attackers were generally wel-
comed by a hail of cannonballs, molten
lead and garbage fired from the tops of
these walls.

The historical upper town still towers
impressively over the harbor to this day
and proves an unforgettable sight for
visitors approaching Eivissa from the sea.
The view of the medieval old town is truly

deserving of the description "picturesque."

From **Mercat Vell** ⑩ and via a stone ramp you'll reach the **★★Portal de Ses Taules** ⑩ which features a drawbridge that wasn't re-hinged until the end of the 20th century. Two headless **Roman statues** flank both sides of the gate: the goddess Juno and a Roman legionnaire. Behind it is the **arms cache** of the guards, these days a rendezvous for lovers. Another Roman sculpture greets you from a nearby niche. Above the Portal de Ses Taules, within the historical walls of the **Baluard de Sant Joan** bastion, the **★Museu d'Art Contemporani** (opened in 1961) exhibits the works of both local and foreign contemporary artists. The vivid white **★Plaça de Vila** ⑪ is pure shopping and strolling territory, a satisfying playground for window-shoppers,

Above: The upper town quarter of Dalt Vila with its 2-kilometer fortress walls has been declared a UNESCO World Heritage site. Right: Lunch break on Plaça de Vila.

those simply wishing to relax, café-goers and avid shoppers and art-hunters; the **Galeria Carl van der Voort** was one of the first galleries on Ibiza to exhibit and sell modern Ibizan art.

On the other side of the square, behind the arms cache, a somewhat wider road ascends to the **★Plaça dels Desamparats** ⑫ which on its higher level is known by the name of **Sa Carossa**. The historic **El Portalón** restaurant and the charming **La Ventana** hotel are located on the right-hand side and are very popular venues, especially with members of the arts métier. A splendid view of Eivissa's new town and the harbor can be enjoyed from its roof terrace, as well as from the town's upper fortress wall. A life-sized bronze sculpture of **Isidor Macabich i Llobet** (1883-1973) is shaded by eucalyptus trees. This much-admired Pitiusan historian carries an open book in his hand which is supposed to represent one edition of the multi-volumed complete works of *Historia de Ibiza*. After the Second World War Macabich brought his en-

tire respect to bear in his effort to have the daily newspaper *Diario de Ibiza* published again.

Dalt Vila is not an open-air museum, but a well-inhabited, quarter of town pulsating with life. Diverse smells and radio sounds overlay one another, children's squabbling and screeching permeates the rising and falling din emanating from the maze of streets, topped by a generous layer of piercing laughter and everyday conversation. The simple and sometimes shabby natural stone houses are so close together that their residents can look right into each other's windows and shake hands across the narrow streets – a shoulder-to-shoulder neighborhood as it has been for two-and-a-half thousand years. Since the 1980s the old town's restoration program has taken a firm hold, but it will take generations to complete. This is a well-preserved piece of the original Ibiza.

Our journey resumes on Plaça de Vila at the end of which, where the steps of **Escala de Pedra** descend, you'll reach the **Plaça del Regente Gotarredona** ⑬

which leads through a densely-populated quarter, beneath and through lines busy with washing and past scrapped gas bottles and jacked-up motorbikes. Restraint with one's camera is called for here – the people living in these modest conditions often don't like being photographed.

Heading about 100 meters east from the Plaça you'll come to a popular vantage point – the ★**Plaça del Sol** ⑭. This square has recently been beautified, a restaurant sets up its tables along the pavement and guests can look beyond the walls onto the old town roofs. A dark gateway leads downward though the meter-thick bastion walls around the **Portal Nou**. This "new gate" was one of the most important accessways to the upper town. From this very spot invaders used to be attacked with concerted defensive power.

A flight of steps leads up to **Carrer Sant Josep**, a street through which even Archduke Ludwig of Habsburg, the first "tourist" on Ibiza, enjoyed strolling at the end of the 19th century; he mentioned this street in his writings. Via another

flight of steps you reach **Carrer de Joan Roman**, one of Dalt Vila's broader streets. On the left-hand side you'll see the façade of a former monastery (*seminari*).

After passing more steps you'll come to the legendary **★El Corsario** ⑮ hotel and restaurant, where many showbusiness greats stayed when tourism on the island was first starting to take off. The hotel's pebbled entrance hall is very beautiful, but the establishment no longer belongs to the premier league; a magnificent view over the city can be enjoyed from its terrace.

At the Corsario, after taking the first turning right and passing through narrow lanes, you'll reach the "main street" **★Carrer Major** lined with souvenir shops and stately old mansions. On its left a slightly winding road ascends to the

Above: Santa Maria de las Nieves in the cathedral succeeded the goddess Tanit (Museo Arqueológic) as patron saint of the island.
Right: Beauty pageant in El Divino.

highest point of Dalt Vila, the **★Plaça de la Catedral**. Here the **★Catedral Mare de Deu de la Neu** ⑯ (*Santa Maria de las Nieves*) looms up into the brilliant blue sky; "Mary of the Snow" – a truly unique name for a church on an island where snow is an alien entity. The site where today's church stands was once occupied by a Roman temple, an Early Christian basilica and a Moorish mosque. The building of this cathedral began in the 13th century and was not completed until 1592. It was originally Gothic as its bell tower and few windows verify, but this fact is barely discernible due to the many alterations carried out since then. Thanks to costly restorations over the last few years it is now possible to view the two choir chapels in the interior, as well as some splendid windows and choir apses. The **★museum** in the vestry holds a monstrance made of pure gold.

Another worthwhile sight next to the cathedral is the **★★Museo Arqueológic d'Eivissa i Formentera** where Carthaginian, Roman, Moorish and

Eivissa

Spanish exhibits, as well as prehistoric finds from the tomb of Ca na Costa (Formentera) are displayed. The **castle** on the other side of the square was once part of the *Almudaina* fortress complex and has had to be reinforced with concrete due to its danger of collapsing. After crossing the lane between the two buildings you come to the **Plaça Almaduina** with the **★Baluard de Sant Bernat** ⑰ bastion on the right-hand side, an impressive part of the fortress wall. The extensive panoramic view from here includes the Phoenician tomb site at Puig de Molins, the sand beaches and the salinas; even Formentera can be made out in the south.

Back on **Carrer Major** continue along the prolongation known as **★Carrer Sant Ciriac** where you'll spot a small chapel by the name of **Capella de Sant Ciriac** ⑱. Its plaque tells the story of a saint named *Ciriac* on whose name day – 8th August (1235) – Christian troops invaded the city which at that time was under Moorish occupation. The **Convent de**

Sant Cristòfol, a simple church with a late Baroque altar, is also located along this road.

Continue back down the main Carrer Major and **Carrer de Santa Maria.** On **Plaça d'Espanya** ⑲ you'll come across the former Dominican monastery complex of *Convent de Sant Domènec* (1592) which was secularized to function as **ajuntament** (town hall) in 1938. In 1986 this former sacral building was altered to suit the requirements of the modern municipal administration: city councillors now attend sessions beneath painted barrel vaults in the former monastery refectory and the cloister presents a striking setting for concerts and exhibitions. Wine-sipping art aficionados, local patriots and residents stroll around viewing vernissages and taking in the aura of this special place which exudes centuries of atmosphere – in other words, a place with a soul. Another remarkable building, the **Can Fajarnés Cardona** – a private residence from the early 20th century – is also located on the Plaça. The former

monastery church of **★Sant Domènec** towers behind the town wall; its domes are tiled and it has some splendid Baroque altars. Adjacent to it is the **Baluard de Santa Llucia ㉑** with a restored **defense tower** from where there is a fine view over Sa Penya and the harbor.

★MARINA D'ES BOTAFOC

The yachting and sports harbor of **★Marina d'Es Botafoc ㉑** occupies the other side of the harbor basin. It represents "modern" Eivissa and the quarter around it is still undergoing development. Its hypermodern architecture, into which traditional local elements have been incorporated, was modeled on Mallorca's Port Portals and Marbella's Puerto Banús. Cafés and top-class restaurants (like the **El Divino** club which is renowned for its highly original parties), sophisticated boutiques (such as that of *ad-lib* fashion

Above: The Aguamar aquatic park in Platja d'En Bossa.

designer **Dora Herbst**) and the new **casino** (tie compulsory!) flank **Passeig Joan Carles I** (Passeig Marítím). Luxury yachts hover offshore. The view of the old town is magnificent from here. The **Pacha** megadisco (behind the casino), "mother of theme parties," is currently opening subsidiaries all over the world.

The old lighthouse of **Far d'Es Botafoc ㉒** is located on the island of **Illa Grossa**. The small **Platja des Duros** (shore of coins) connects the peninsula of **Illa Plana** with the lighthouse island. A swimming competition is held from here to the lighthouse at the end of July/beginning of August to celebrate the *Fiesta de Nuestra Senora de las Nieves* (a festival honoring the patron saint of Eivissa). Enthusiastic sailors can charter a boat or yacht on the harbor's northern side.

Platja de Talamanca ㉓, a quiet hotel zone, is located on the other side of the cape. The hills behind it are occupied by villas – Eivissa's most expensive residential area, in fact. Those living here are privileged with fine views over Dalt Vila.

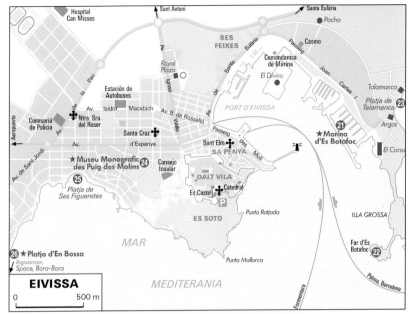

EIVISSA
0   500 m

★PUIG DES MOLINS

This rather inconspicuous hill just below the town wall forms the nucleus of the city. This is where the Carthaginians chose to build a necropolis for their dead and where the legendary figure Hannibal is said to have stayed while engrossed in dialogue with his ancestors.

The ★**Museu Monografic del Puig des Molins** ㉔ (Via Romana 31), Ibiza's most important museum, preserves many archaic legacies. Most of the island's Carthaginian finds are on display here and experts consider these collections, which date back to Punic times, to be the most important ever excavated around the Mediterranean. The most attractive are the depictions of *Tanit*, beneath which you'll see a beautiful bust from a cave at Cala Sant Vicent. There are also terra cotta figures found by shepherds in a mountain cave near Sant Joan, coins and jewelry from the Can Sora necropolis at Cala d'Hort, ostrich eggs and statuettes from La Plana island opposite the modern

harbor of Botafoc, sarcophagi from the necropolis of Can Berri d'en Sargent near Sant Josep, as well as ritual implements and weapons from over 3,000 **burial chambers** carved into the cliffs. Some of these rock chambers can be seen from the museum grounds; the museum itself is currently closed for renovation.

★PLATJA D'EN BOSSA

Eivissa's beaches are located in the south, not far from the city. The **Platja de Ses Figueretes** ㉕, just behind Dalt Vila and flanked by faceless but good-value accommodation, bars and restaurants, is still within the city boundaries. This shadeless, narrow, 400-meter sand strip is bound by a promenade and teems at night with traders selling daring textiles and unusual souvenirs.

★**Platja d'en Bossa** ㉖ is the island's longest sand beach and extends for 3 kilometers. From early afternoon onward it is almost always occupied by noisy, active young people. It is completely built up

and is enclosed by hotels (including a Club Med), restaurants and supermarkets. Airplanes thunder overhead at short intervals, not bothering the young holidaymakers in the slightest. A hippie market takes place here every Friday in high season.

Platja d'En Bossa has white, fine-grained sand and has a very shallow gradient, meaning that it is also suitable for families with children. Kids can also enjoy an energetic romp in the **Aguamar** fun pool which has some huge water slides and an adventure playground. The "bigger kids" can enjoy a rave next door in the popular daytime disco **Space** or in the trendy beach disco **Bora-Bora** (with bar and restaurant) – all beneath the airport's flight path. Conclusion: sun, sand, and an energetic clientele out to have a good time. Those seeking tranquility will have come to the wrong place, but "plane spotters" will be in their element.

Above: Punic terra-cotta figurines on display in the Museu Archeológic (Dalt Vila).

EIVISSA

Oficina de Información y Turismo (Tourist Information Office), Passeig Vara de Rey 13, tel. 971-301900 and 315131; **Oficina de Información Turistica**, Carrer Antoni Riquer 2, tel. 301900, fax 301562.

The international airport **Aeroport d'Eivissa** is located 7 km southwest of Eivissa, behind Sant Jordi. Buses run from the airport to the city hourly between 7:30 am and 10:30 pm.

☺☺☺ **Club Don Toni**, Platja d'en Bossa, tel. 971-305012, fax 305803; one of the larger hotels on the popular beach, large swimming pool, extensive in-house sports facilities.

Royal Plaza, C/. Pedro Francés, tel. 971-313711, fax 314095; modern, ocher building, dark furnishings.

Ocean Drive, Marina Botafoch, tel. 971-318112, fax 312228, e-mail odrive@step.es; Art-Deco style building with tastefully-furnished rooms.

La Torre del Canónigo, C/. Major 8, tel. 971-303884, fax 307843; luxurious apartment hotel popular with fashion jet-setters.

El Palacio, Carrer de la Conquesta 2, tel. 971-301478, fax 391581. Small, luxury hotel in Dalt Vila, has seen many famous stars, rather kitschy interior.

La Ventana, Sa Carroca 13, tel. 971-390857, fax 390145; not the best, but the most beautifully-situated hotel in Eivissa; formerly a manor, located just below the bastion of Santa Llúcia in the historic upper town.

☺☺ **Los Molinos**, C/. Ramón Muntaner 60, tel. 971-302254, fax 302504; open all year, between the city and Platja d'en Bossa.

Argos, Platja de Talamanca, tel. 971-312126, fax 316201; family hotel directly on the beach, with childcare and entertainment.

El Corsario, C/. Ponent 5, tel. 971-301248, fax 390953; old pirates' palace with a panoramic view and charming garden terrace.

Rio, Passeig Maritim, tel. 971-190404, fax 313900; striking apartment hotel on the edge of Eivissa.

Roberto Playa, C/. Galícia 22, tel. 971-390421, fax 390826; small, recently-opened hotel in the Figueretes quarter.

☺ **Hostal Parque**, Miquel Cayetà Soler s/n, tel. 971-301358; simple *hostal* in city center, lovely view of Dalt Vila from some rooms. **Marina**, C/. Barcelona 7, tel. 971-310172; simple and clean *hostal* at the harbor, run by old-established family. **Europa Púnico**, C/. Aragón 28, tel. 971-303428; basic *hostal* in new town.

Montesol, Passeig Vara de Rey 2, tel. 971-310161; oldest hotel on the island (1934) in lovely location, restored.

Delfin Verde, C/. Garijo 2, tel. 971-310215; nostalgic classic in the harbor quarter, the cuisine here blends Spanish and Italian influences; seafood specialties. **El Olivo**, Plaça de Vila 7-9, tel. 971-300680; in the center of the old town, top-class French cuisine, sophisticated meat dishes, suitable dress required. **Bar Juan**, Carrer Montgrí 8, tel. 971-310766; small, inexpensive bar in center of old town, good home cooking. **El Portalon**, Plaça dels Desamparats s/n, tel. 971-303901; Spanish food in stylish city palazzo in Dalt Vila. **El Principe**, Ses Figueretes, Passeig Maritim, tel. 971-301914; international cuisine, restaurant with garden section and lovely sea views. **S'Oficina**, Av. Espanya 6, tel. 971-300016; an "office" (*oficina*) for business people (who always know where the best food is served). **Bar Bahía**, C/. Garijo 1, tel. 311019; source of nutrition for Ibiza veterans, delicious roast chicken. **Can Alfredo**, Passeig Vara de Rey 16, tel. 971-311274; one of the best restaurants on the Pitiusas since 1934, famous for paella and fish. **Celler Baleares**, Av. Ignacio Wallis 18, tel. 971-311965; rustic, good tapas and island specialties. **El Faro**, Plaça de Sa Riba 2, tel. 971-311153; superb seafood with fine view of harbor. **Sa Caldera**, Bisbe Pare Huix 19, tel. 971-306416; seafood restaurant popular with Spaniards, in Eivissa's new town. **Victoria**, C/. Riambau 1; brimming with locals, home cooking, inexpensive. **Brasero**, Es Passadis 4, tel. 971-311469; excellent French cuisine, delicious starters. **Avenida**, Av. Bartolomen de Roselló 113, tel. 971-314270; simple decor, good meat dishes and oven-roasted fish. **Beda's La Scala**, C/. Sa Carossa 7, tel. 971-300383; Swiss culinary art in romantic Dalt Vila villa. **El Rubio**, Plaça de sa Riba 7, tel. 971-310071; Swiss cuisine and Italian pasta. **Café Sidney**, Botafoc yacht harbor, tel. 971-192243; trendy bar serving food all day, popular Sunday brunch, good German beer. **La Brasa**, C/. Pere Sala 3, tel. 971-301202; restaurant with beautiful garden serving Catalan and Ibizan specialties and grilled meats. *CAFÉS:* **Bar Mar y Sol**, Carrer Lluis Tur y Palau 1; trendy café at the harbor, excellent observation point. **Montesol**, Passeig Vara de Rey 2; oldest café in town, yet another good observation point. **Café/Bar Madagascar**, Plaça des Parc s/n; here you can sit beneath shady trees and overlook the upper town. **Sunset Café**, Plaça des Parc s/n; café by day, hot-spot by night. **Parque Bar**, Plaça des Parc s/n; fashionable bar, lots of wicker chairs, on the square. **Bar Tolo**, Avgda. d'Espanya 8; pleasant breakfast bar, *tapas* and *bocadillos*. **Café de Viena**, Avgda. d'Espana 8; Vienna-style café, good service. **Es Molins Bar,** Avgda. d'Espanya 35; whilst eating their snacks the locals debate the newspapers over the noise of the tv on the ceiling. **The Mezzanine Bar**, Paseo Marítimo, tel. 310876; internet café.

Teatro Perreira, Carrer Conde Rosellón; live blues and jazz. Its café is very popular for breakfast (from 10 am). **Bar Incognito**, C/. Santa Llúcia 47; incognito isn't quite the right description, but you can always pretend. **Bar JJ**, C/. Mare de Déu 79; *the* place to get chatted up, popular with gay people. **Bar Questions**, C/. Mare de Déu 79; seedy bar. **Dome**, C/. Barcelona; a meeting-place for eccentrics. **Keeper**, Paseo Marítimo s/n; popular bar to get you in the mood for the long night ahead. **Blue Rose**, in Ses Figueretes, C./Navarra 27, nightclub with striptease show.

Pacha, new harbor, Passeig Perimetral, tel. 971-310959, huge disco with three floors each with different music, restaurant, 18 bars and VIP area; open from midnight, also open Fri and Sat in winter. **El Divino**, Marina d'Es Botafoc, just before the casino, tel. 971-190177, stylish disco with originally-designed restaurant and terrace, lovely view of old town. **Space**, Platja d'En Bossa, tel. 971-396793, disco that doesn't open til morning (for people who think midnight is far too early to be going out) therefore a daytime club. **Amnesia**, road to Sant Antoni, after 6 km (near Sant Rafel), tel. 971-191041; huge disco with capacity for 5,000, two dance floors, best DJs from Europe. **Privilege**, road to Sant Antoni, 7 km (near Sant Rafel), tel. 971-198160; megadisco with capacity for up to 10,000 guests.

Museu Monografic des Puig des Molins, Vía Romana 31, Tue-Sat 10 am-1 pm and 4-7 pm; outstanding collection of Phoenician-Carthaginian finds; closed for renovation; guided tours to the burial chambers of the Carthaginian necropolis. **Museu Arqueològic d'Eivissa I Formentera**, Plaça de la Catedral, Mon-Sat 10 am-1 pm and 4-7 pm; the history of Ibiza and Formentera are graphically illustrated here – from the age of the hunter-gatherer right up to the arrival of the Spanish. **Museu d'Art Contemporani**, Portal de ses Taules, Mon-Sat 10 am-1 pm and 5-8 pm; contemporary art by local and international artists.

Dora Herbst, Marina de Botafoc, Local 315; the owner is one of the trend-setters of Ibizan fashion, exclusive designs. **Paula's**, Sa Penya, C/. de la Virgen 4; unusual creations by Stuart Rudnick and Armin Heinemann. **Boom-Bastic**, Dalt Vila, Carrer Major; fun beachwear. Goldi, C/. Conde de Rosellón 10, gold and silver jewelry, own designs. **Mercat Nou**, C/. Extremadura; over 50 stalls offer fresh goods in the new market hall – fruit, veg and fresh fish. **Es Moli d'Or**, Av. Macabich 39; French bakery, baguette, croissants, fine cake and French wine. **Quefa**, C/. Cayetano Soler 9; German and French delicatessen, large range of wines, also bistro with warm and cold dishes. **S'Oliver**, C/. Pere Sala 3, tel. 971-392569; tasteful interior, plants, gifts.

SOUTH AND WEST

SOUTH COAST
SANT JOSEP
ES VEDRA
WEST COAST
SANT ANTONI
SANTA AGNÈS
SANT RAFEL

South and west

THE SOUTH COAST

Due to the building of the airport the town of **Sant Jordi** ➊, directly behind Eivissa's southern periphery, expanded far too quickly. Yet the church of ***Església de Sant Jordi** (1577) still towers up from the midst of the unsightly buildings; it is possibly the most impressive of the 23 fortress churches on the island. This structure features a vestibule with three arches and an exposed belfry above the portal. The sacral building is crowned by battlements and gives a cold and unyielding impression: a clear indication of just how much emphasis was placed on fortifying oneself against one's enemies in those days. Enthusiastic punters can place bets on the horse races at the **Hipódromo** on Sunday nights.

The small village of **Sant Francesc** ➋ is still untouched by mass tourism. Its atmosphere is rustic and its roads are narrow and sun-scorched. A few houses are clustered around its little church.

The ****Ses Salines** ➌ salt flats, laid out like a chess board, extend behind the town across an area of 500 hectares and as far as **Puig des Falcó**. The Carthaginians already made use of these *salinas* in early times, as did the Romans and Arabs in

Left: The coast near Sa Caleta.

later periods. The Ibicencos still export tens of thousands of tons of salt to northern Europe. Although the huge, white-grained, shimmering expanse is under private company ownership, natives arriving by car show no scruples in helping themselves to the salt between Sa Canal and the sand beach of Es Cavallet by shoveling it into containers and bags they have conveniently brought with them.

The southern tip of Ibiza isn't just a paradise for swimmers, but also for nature lovers who appreciate the salinas wetlands. This nature reserve is the home of ospreys, lizards and flora which thrives in a saline environment. Right in the middle of the salinas a road leads east to the ***Es Cavallet** ➍ naturist beach which is under conservation because of its fine, pine-lined dunes. It has officially been set aside as a nudist beach and is also the hub of the gay community.

The ***Platja de Ses Salines** ➎ (*Platja de Migjorn*) is also located nearby. This part-sand, part-rock, 1.5-kilometer beach is flanked by dunes, maritime pines and juniper trees. This happens to be a "mega-cool" beach and is accordingly well-frequented by socialites blessed with beautiful bodies who like to congregate in the **Malibú** beach bar; this is a trendy beach, with service. Party people still exhausted from the night before sunbathe in front of

the small **Bar Sa Trincha** and loudspeakers emit thumping house beats.

Next to it, in the harbor of **Sa Canal**, the salt that has been extracted from evaporated seawater is loaded onto ships.

A road circumventing the town and passing some small rocky inlets leads to the tip of the small peninsula – the **Punta de ses Portes ❻** with its mighty, 16th-century **Torre de ses Portes** defense tower. From here you can see part of Eivissa's old town, the shipping traffic and even the islands of **Espalmador** and **Espardell**, both with prominent lighthouses.

West of the airport the pebble beach of **Platja d'Es Codolar** and the small rock and sand bay of **★Sa Caleta ❼** adjoining it beckon. Sa Caleta is surrounded by steep, reddish-brown cliffs, so shoes will be necessary.

Above: Esglèsia de Sant Jordi is one of the most impressive fortress churches on the island. Right: Trendy meeting place at Platja de Ses Salines – Bar Sa Trincha.

The foundations of the 2,700-year-old Punic settlement of **Poblat Fenici** were excavated on the neighboring peninsula, behind which the tiny, secluded bay of **El Rincón del Marino** lies well hidden.

The **★Cala Jondal ❽** is one of the larger bays here. Its rather narrow beach has a seafood restaurant, but there are only a few short stretches of sand between the masses of pebbles. Nevertheless, the sheltered bay is very popular with families as the projecting high cliffs form a barrier against the wind and high waves and there are also plenty of shady pines, making it an ideal place for children.

The boatyards of this former fishing town can still be seen in the wide, neighboring bay of **Porroig** (*Port Roig*).

Cova Santa ❾, or holy cave, is the name of a small stalactite cave located near the main road from Eivissa to Sant Josep and is open for viewing until noon. It is said to have once served as a place of refuge for the Ibicencos during pirate raids.

Map p. 34-35, Guidepost p. 44-45

*SANT JOSEP DE SA TALAIA

*Sant Josep ❿ is a little showpiece town and with a population of 12,000 it is the main town in this region – the largest on the island in terms of area. Here one can get an idea of how the islanders might picture the result of the restoration of their "old" Ibiza: local island traditions are kept alive by many folk dancing groups; the church and buildings bordering the town, main road and surrounding green areas have been exemplarily restored. The supermarkets, banks, post office and medical facilities are, however, representative of modern Ibiza. Sant Josep is supposedly the richest town on the island and has developed into a service center for the region from Platja d'en Bossa with its salt flats, the south coast with Es Cubells and the west coast with its many beaches and bays, to shortly before Sant Antoni.

The *Esglesia de Sant Josep church which dates back to 1731 is a large fortress church. The village square in front of it is considered Ibiza's most beautiful **Plaça**, but in Roman times it served as an execution square. The olive tree with a bench beneath it is reputed to be about 1,200 years old. The interior of the church, with the standard three arches leading to the vestibule, is dominated by a richly-adorned Baroque altar with a statue of Joseph, a carved pulpit dating back to 1763 and numerous artworks and valuable glass windows featuring the shepherds' worship and Christophorus with Jesus. The altar was damaged during the Spanish Civil War (1936-39), after which the women of Sant Josep parted with their jewelry so that the holy table could once again be plated in gold.

Both locals and tourists like to meet up in the **Bernet Vinya** bar. Another original café here, with a beautiful interior courtyard and a cultural program, is the **Raco Verd**.

There is a fine panoramic view from ****Sa Talaia** ⓫ – Ibiza's highest elevation at 475 meters; on days when visibility is good you can even make out the coastline of the Spanish mainland. A gravel road west of Sant Josep leads to a summit crowned by a transmitter mast; the ascent on foot via the direct hiking route from the town center takes about 2 hours and leads you first past olive trees and vines, then through pines and sabina jumipers.

*Es Cubells

*Es Cubells ⓬ on the steep southern coast is a relatively new village. It sits atop a high cliff and was therefore never suitable as a settlement for fishermen or farmers. In 1855 the Carmelite monk and mystic Francisco Palau selected this as a home for himself and his followers. He later withdrew to the small island of Es Vedrà, alone. The hermitage he founded, **Seminari d'Es Cubells**, still practises spiritual rituals in which foreigners may also partipicate. By contrast, the lookout terrace at the **Llumbi** village bar attracts day-trippers who prefer to have spirit in their drinks. A little road winds its way down to the small beach of **Platja d'Es Cubells**.

Several more excursions can be made from Es Cubells, for example to the nearby beach **Platja de ses Boques** (with a restaurant) or a 3-kilometers hike further south to the bay of **Cala Llentrisca**, ideal for swimming.

**ES VEDRÀ AND ES VEDRANELL

When viewed from ***Mirador d'Es Savinar** ⓭ (near the Torre del Pirata) the description "mysterious – like a sleeping dragon" appears fitting for these two legendary islets glowing in the afternoon sunlight.

Depending on the incidence of light and the mood of the sea the island of **Es Vedrà** ⓮, a 382-meter-high cliff, sometimes resembles a ship in foaming waters. Some say the island is cursed; this mere half-square-kilometer islet is steeped in

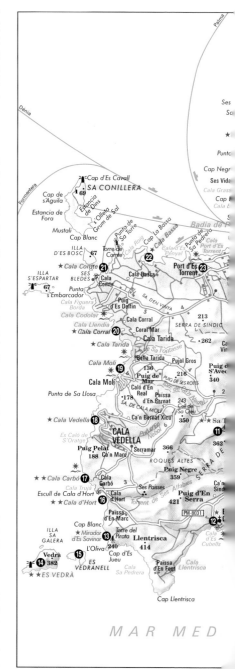

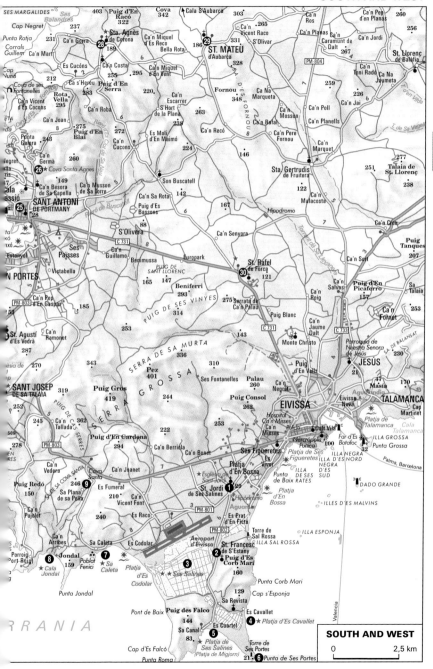

SES MARGALIDES · Ses Balandres
Cap Negret
Punta Rotja 231 · Can Gurra
Corrals Guillem · Ca'n Marí
Es Cucóns
Cap Nunó 212 · Ca s'Hereu
Cova de ses Fontanelles
Ca'n Vicent d'Es Cocons
Rota Vella 295 · Ca'n Roba
Punta Galera 249 · Ca'n Joan 8
Ca'n Germà 260
Cova Santa Agnes
Ca'n Besora de Sa Capella 149
Ca'n Musson de Sa Torre

403 · Puig d'En Racó 322
Cova 342 · Cala S'Aubarca 303
Sta. Agnès de Corona 237
Ca'n Miquel d'Es Reco · Bella Rota
186 · St. MATEU d'Aubarca
331 · S'Olivar
Puig d'En Serra 283 255 295
Ca'n Miquel d'En Vent 328
Ca'n Costa 220
Fornou 348
Ca'n Marqueta
Ca'n Escarrer · S'Hort de la Plana 238
Ca'n Recó
263
Puig d'En Blai 275
272 · Ca'n Cucons
Es Molí d'En Maimó 224
146

Son Buscatell
Ca'n Sa Rota 142
Puig d'Es Bassons
167
Hipodromo

265 · Vicent Raco
Ca'n Ros
Ca'n Planas 256 260
Caramunt de Dalt 267
Ca'n Toni Radò · Ca Na Jaumeta
259 226
Ca'n Jai
Ca'n Poll · Ca'n Planells
Ca'n Rafal
Ca'n Mosson
Ca'n Pere Fornou
Sta. Gertrudis de Fruitera 122
Ca'n Malacosta 251
Talaia de St. Llorenç 238

St. Llorenç de Balàfia
Ca'n Jordi

PM-804

I. de Sa Vegeta
Ca'n Marquet 277

SANT ANTONI DE PORTMANY 28
S'Olivera
Ses Païsses
Vistabella
Can Guillamo
Benimussa
C 731 88

Ca'n Senyora
St. Rafel de Força 121
PUIG DE SANT LLORENÇ
Europark
Beniferri 293
165 147
Serrata de Ca'n Palau
Puig d'Es Vinyes 314 275
Puig Blanc
143
Monte Christo
Parroquia de Nuestra Senora de Jesús
JESÚS 21
Masía 47
230 170
TALAMANCA

Ca'n Sort
Puig Tanques 207
Ca'n Roig
Ca'n Salvos
Puig d'En Picaferro 157
Ca'n Jaume Dalt
C 731
C 733
SA BALANSAT
Ca'n Fornet 253
Sa Talaia
Ca'n Creu

N PORTES
Ca'n Rep d'En Gaspar
PM-803
58 185
St. Agustí d'Es Vedrà 287
270
SANT JOSEP DE SA TALAIA
319
245
278
PM-803
Ca'n Tallada 362
Puig d'En Cardona 294
Ca'n Berríola
Ca'n Bonet
Ca'n Jaanet
Ca'n Vedora

343
Pez 401
SERRA DE SA MURTA
336
SERRA GROSSA
Puig Gros 419
244
253
222

310
Ses Fontanelles
Palau 260
Puig Consol 262
Ca'n Negret
253

Puig d'En Valls
EIVISSA
Hospital Can't Misses
Ca'n Misses
Policia
Dalt Vila
Necròpolis Punica
100
Ses Figueretes
Es Vivot
Platja de Ses Figueretes
Punta de Ses Rates
Eivissa Nova
Eivissa Indio
Platja de Talamanca
Cala Talamanca
ILLA GROSSA
Far d'Es Botafoc
Punta Grossa 32
ILLA NEGRA
ILLA D'ES NORD
ILLA NEGRA D'ES SUD
Palma, Barcelona

Cap Martinet

DADO GRANDE
ILLES D'ES MALVINS

Puig Redó 150
Sa Plana de sa Pella 246
Ca'n Pujolet
240
Es Funeral
210
Ca'n Vicent Font
Es Racó
Es Codolar
PM-801
PM-802
Torre de Sal Rossa
Ca'n Arribes
Jondal 159
Poblat Fenici
Sa Caleta
Es Cartell
Platja d'Es Codolar
Ses Salines
Punta Jondal

St. Jordi de Ses Salines 29
Hipódromo
Aguamar
Platja d'En Bossa
Es Prat d'En Ficta
Aeroport d'Eivissa
St. Francesc de S'Estany
Puig d'Es Corb Marí 160
129 Sa Revista
Es Cuártel
Pont de Baix
Puig des Falco 144
Sa Canal 83
Platja de Ses Salines (Platja de Migjorn)
Cap d'Es Falcó
Punta Roma

ILLA SAL ROSSA
ILLA ESPONJA
Platja d'En Bossa
Punta Corb Marí
Cap s'Esponja
Es Cavallet
Platja d'Es Cavallet
Torre de Ses Portes
21 Punta de Ses Portes

Valencia

RRANIA

Cala Jondal
Port Roig
Porroig

SOUTH AND WEST
0   2,5 km

myths and immersed in legends, and innumerable vessels have gone down off its
shores. The cause for this is said to be a
mysterious energy field which pulls the
boats downward and even causes unfortu-
nate carrier pigeons to never return home
again; this is supposedly caused by the
Bermuda Triangle's opposite magnetic
pole. UFOs have also been sighted here;
Erich von Däniken even located aliens'
landing strips in the right-angled lines of
the cliffs.

Es Vedranell ⓯ is only a small, offshore islet dominated by falcons, seagulls
and other species that like to nest here.

Even today esoterics from all over are
magically drawn to both islets, which
some believe to be the remains of the lost
kingdom of Atlantis. Excursion boats
from Cala d'Hort (and other harbors)
head for the mystery island of Es Vedrà.

*Above: The road to Mirador d'Es Savinar is
fringed by bushes of flowering thyme in
springtime. Right: View of Es Vedra from Cala
d'Hort.*

THE WEST COAST

The entire southwestern coastal region
is scenically impressive, with alternating
blue bays, green hills and red cliffs. However, the tentacles of tourism have nevertheless gained a strong grip here in the
form of unsightly hotel complexes and
bungalow settlements.

**Cala d'Hort ⓰ is considered by
many Ibiza connoisseurs to be the most
beautiful bay on the island. Its narrow
sand and pebble beach has a very romantic aura in late afternoon when Es Vedrà
shimmers like an enchanted islet.

In 1985 a Punic-Roman settlement
with cisterns and burial tombs – **Ses
Paisses** – was discovered nearby. The
Carthaginians founded it in the 5th century B.C. and it was extended further by
the Romans in the 2nd century B.C. Later
and until the 7th century A.D. it fell into
Byzantine hands.

The small, flat sand bay of ****Cala
Carbó** ⓱ is only accessible via a dusty
road sprinkled with potholes; it has two

small beach restaurants, making it a hot insider tip.

The surrounding area is quite well inhabited and encompasses the fjord-like bay of **★Cala Vedella** ⓲ with its clear blue water, bars and restaurants, **Cala Moli** ⓳ which is framed by cliffs and boasts wonderfully romantic sunsets and **★Cala Tarida** which offers plenty of white sand and wonderful crystal-clear water. These once-idyllic bays are still partly fringed by pine forests, juniper trees and orchids, but the development of the region proved excessive and the vast numbers of hotels and vacation houses, coupled with frantic trade, are a major thorn in the side of the locals.

The string of bays which includes **★Cala Corral** ⓴, **Cala Llendia** and **Cala Codolar** with their narrow pebble-and-sand beaches is far from the asphalted roads and very peaceful. It is their charming, natural setting that makes them so special. Small holiday settlements have attempted to blend in with the landscape here. A zigzag trail leads hikers high

above the coast through a rich variety of *macchia* vegetation, past aleppo pines, ollastre, wild olives and white rockrose. Kermes oaks, with their distinctively shiny, spiny green leaves, also thrive here.

There are several hotel-free bays near **★Cala Comte** ㉑ which are still surrounded by a relatively pristine natural environment: sand dunes, beach pines and beautiful cliffs. A lovely view of the offshore islands can be enjoyed from these shores. The largest island in the distance, **Sa Conillera**, can be reached by excursion boats which run from Cala Bassa and Sant Antoni. The bay is ideal for children to play and paddle, as there are many shallow spots.

★Cala Bassa ㉒ is another fine sand bay which is flat, well-frequented and ideal for children. Its pretty beach is shaded by groups of pines and *sabina* trees. There are numerous bars and a wide range of water sports.

The once-beautiful sand beach of **Port d'es Torrent** ㉓ is today lined along its entire length with hotels which are

booked mainly by British tourists. A culinary ray of hope is provided by **Rick's Café**.

Sant Agustì d'Es Vedrà ㉔ south of Sant Antoni, is said to be Ibiza's oldest village. Some consider the mix of houses sprinkled over the hill – traditional as well as modern buildings – to be the most beautifully-situated settlement on Ibiza. The town is surrounded by terraced fields of almond trees, agaves and orange trees. The focal point of the tiny **Plaça Mayor** is its small, fortress-like **church** beside which the local Berri family manages an art gallery, a bar and the stylish Ibizan restaurant **Can Berri Vel**l, located in a very old farmhouse. The Colegio Alemán school for the children of immigrants – not only Germans as its name suggests – in the *Can Blau* (blue roof) building is the only one of its kind on the Balearics.

Above: Rust-colored rocks, luminious sand and clean, turquoise waters – welcome to Cala Comte. Right: Sant Antoni de Portmany can accommodate 200,000 holidaymakers.

SANT ANTONI DE PORTMANY

For a long time Ibiza's western coast remained a sleepy and idyllic corner, at least until British tourists arrived 35 years ago and put an end to the tranquility. The once-peaceful fishing village of **Sant Antoni de Portmany** ㉕ quickly mutated into the hub of Ibiza's cost-conscious package tourism industry with more than one hundred hotels and apartment complexes, bars, souvenir shops, bureaux de change, fish'n'chip shops and discotheques. In summer its 14,000 inhabitants are joined by over 200,000 tourists. Even its white parish church – once the focal point of the village – has been surrounded by faceless constructions. And the former harbor as well as part of the sea have been cemented over to make more room for the seasonal guests. Noise, shouting and street riots monitored by the police now dominate its nocturnal atmosphere.

A powerful tour de force was necessary to change Sant Antoni's image and dispose of its ugliest architectural sores. But

the town's location, with its beautiful sunsets and surroundings bays, compensates for many of the visual features that couldn't be repaired. With its jagged cliffs, gentle dunes and fine beaches this town is an ideal point of departure for coastal explorations and also for investigating the furrowed hillscapes inland.

Sant Antoni's residents, many of them fishing families, have managed to "reclaim" their town; the men can once again be seen mending their nets at the harbor mole and the newly-designed, palm-lined promenade ★**Passeig de Ses Fonts** ❶ will seduce you into taking a stroll and resting on one of its many park benches or relaxing café terraces. The visual extravagance of elegant yachts in the harbor basin is balanced somewhat by local fishing fleets. The bay of Portmany – a true paradise for windsurfers and sailors – was originally part of the best of what Ibiza had to offer, at least until the hotel building boom struck in the 1960s.

The Romans imperiously named the bay *Portus Magnus*, or "Large Port," yet Sant Antoni never shared Eivissa's historical importance because this town of relatively flat hilltops could not be fortified properly and its bay, carved deeply into the west coast, could not offer ships a safe haven. Its harbor, surpassing Eivissa's in both scope and quay length but certainly not regarding protection from the elements, remains exposed to storms sweeping in from the northwest in winter. In high season ferries to the mainland via Formentera and Dénia depart from here.

The **Monument Al Pescador** near the bus stop on Passeig de Ses Fonts recalls the days when this place was inhabited by only a handful of fishermen. At the main junction near the traffic circle you'll see another sculpture: the ★**egg of Columbus** ❷ (*Ou den Colom*) with his caravel – the Santa María – in its hollowed-out core; a work completed in 1992 by local artist Julio Bauzá.

Sant Antoni's historical center is small. The 17th-century **Sant Antoni Abat** ❸ church stands on the remains of a mosque from the Moorish period. The single-

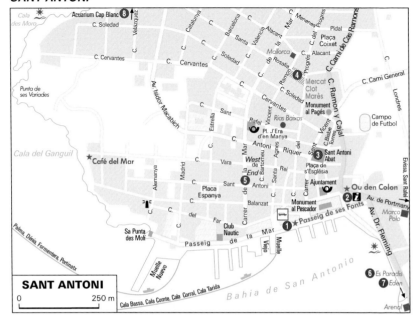

SANT ANTONI

0   250 m

naved building was converted into a fortress and adorned not with religious symbols but with cannons. There is still a cistern in the vestibule from which those locked in could obtain water. This austere house of god is decorated inside with a classical altarpiece depicting St. Anthony. The **Plaça de S'Església** church square, by contrast, is very pretty indeed and surrounded by bars and restaurants.

The Centro Comercial is located nearby and the town's 14,000 residents are extremely proud of their market hall, **Es Mercat Clot Marès** ❹, where one can stock up on foodstuffs of the freshest quality.

Noisy tourism was pushed aside into the so-called **West End**, a small quarter in the old town between the **Carrer de la Mar** ❺ and **Carrer Sant Vicent** where there are a multitude of bars and the beer

Right: Sant Antoni Abat, a fortress church built over Moorish foundations, with a large forecourt and a cistern providing an emergency water supply in case of sieges.

flows in rivers – a fact much appreciated by young British tourists. Loud outdoor music is now prohibited and with regular controls the police ensure this law is adhered to, while at the same time keeping the infamous hooliganism under control. The atmosphere in ★**Café del Mar** further west along **Cala del Ganguil**, where you can watch the sun set whilst sipping a *Sundowner* accompanied by music to get you in the mood, is far more civilized.

Disco-goers will be spoilt in Sant Antoni – the huge dance temples are all within the town instead of outside it, as is the case in the capital, and they also charge lower entrance fees. ★**Es Paradis Terrenal** ❻ has been a popular winner for over 25 years and this huge pyramidal disco with several dance floors, pavilions and plenty of subtropical vegetation can be found along Avinguda Dr. Fleming, which is invaded by party animals every night in peak season. The **Eden** ❼ disco on the same street attracts a younger clientele with its powerful 80,000-watt sound system.

A natural aquarium can be explored north of Sant Antoni: you can admire the ★**Acuarium Cap Blanch** ❽ from a wooden walkway. This natural, artifically-lit sea grotto is home to rays, sea turtles and Mediterranean fish species in all shapes, sizes and colors.

Beaches

During the day excursion buses and boats ferry throngs of vacationers from Passeig de Ses Fonts to the beaches of **Badia de Portmany** (which is actually the bay of Sant Antoni), the extremely popular beaches of **Port d'Es Torrent** or **Cala Bassa** and further on to **Cala Comte, Cala Corral** and **Cala Tarida**. The bustling **Cala des Moro** and the sandy **Cala Gració** are located on the northern side of the bay. Just beyond and further north the unspoilt, sandy bay of ★**Cala Salada** beckons with its clear, turquoise-colored waters which make it an ideal playground for both swimmers and snorkelers.

★Cova Santa Agnès

The sacred cave of ★**Cova Santa Agnès** ㉖, situated 2 kilometers from the center of Sant Antoni and accessible along the Carretera Cas Ramons in a northerly direction, is surrounded by myth and magic. When the Moors ruled Ibiza during the time of the Christian persecution it is reputed to have served as an underground chapel and refuge. It has actually been historically proven that an altar really did once stand here and, until the mid-19th century, the population congregated here to celebrate the feast day of Saint Ines (Santa Agnès in Catalan) with music and dancing.

Legend has it that a shipwrecked aristocrat who had to be rescued from heavy seas donated a portrait of Saint Ines to the local community. When the church had been completed the portrait ceremoniously changed hands, but subsequently mysteriously disappeared from the church several times before turning up in the cave chapel. Eventually the bishop

gave up and declared that church ceremonies should continue in the holy cave. They were not held in the fortress church until the cave chapel's danger of collapsing appeared imminent, after which it fell into oblivion. It was rediscovered in 1972 when archaeologists found ritual implements from the Punic, Roman and Islamic periods. Since then the walls and ceiling of the underground chapel have been satisfactorily reinforced so that a ceremony can be held every year on August 24.

Cap Nunó ㉗ towers 260 meters out of the sea 7 kilometers north of Sant Antoni and is worth hiking to. To its south is **Cova de Ses Fontanellas**, which is not a cave but a glass-covered cliff projection with barely-discernible rock paintings from the Bronze Age.

Above: Finca (west of Santa Agnès de Corona) in typical Ibicenco cubic style which inspired many an architect in the 20th century. Right: The rural face of Ibiza near Sant Mateu d'Aubarca.

*SANTA AGNÈS DE CORONA

When the almond trees blossom (end of December until February) ***Santa Agnès de Corona** ㉘ is undoubtedly the most charming place on Ibiza. In those months the village is enshrouded in a veil of shimmering white, as though snow must have fallen in temperatures of up to 20 degrees. But it isn't snow that surrounds the village, but a sea of flowering almond trees. Residents and locals sit in the **Can Cosmi** bar for hours just appreciating the expansive view of flowering almond valleys, pitying their friends and relatives in the "far north" (which, in their opinion, begins at the Spanish Pyrenees). This village is truly tiny and only has a small square, a few white houses, a simple, early 19th-century **church** and the bar with its popular terrace. Pretty, country accommodation can be found 3 kilometers outside the village in the comfortable *agroturismo* hotel **Can Pujolet**.

From **Santa Agnès** one can partake in some beautiful hikes past fieldstone-

fringed grainfields interspersed with fig trees, their crowns heavy with fruit, olive groves and fields of lavender. Here Ibiza still seems rural, authentic and unspoilt by tourism. Continuing westward you'll reach **Cap Negret**, the dramatically steep coast with the bay of **Ses Balandres** and the offshore rocky islets of **Ses Margalides**.

The most picturesque hiking route is the 6-kilometer, gently-rolling trail eastward to the vine-growing village of **Sant Mateu d'Aubarca ㉙**. You'll be rewarded en route with sweeping views over the untouched valley between the two towns. And along this trail you'll also discover several scattered, unusual constructions: holes in the ground up to three meters deep and wide, lined with rocks. These are the ovens in which limestone used to be burnt, which was then used for whitewashing the houses.

Paredes – tightly-adjoining fieldstones layered over one another which have been used to stop the progression of erosion since time immemorial and common all over Ibiza – can also be seen here, especially in the many terraced vineyards. In winter when sudden and torrential rains cascade from the heavens the earth in some higher regions can get washed away, but these stone barriers then provide some resistance. The lines of *paredes* extend across the island like lifelines, crossing and cuting through each other, following mountain ranges and marking entire hillscapes. Their combined length is estimated to be 10,000 kilometers and they are approximately 1,000 years old.

From Sant Mateu you can hike a further 4 kilometers via Can Pereta to the romantic rocky bay of **Cala S'Aubarca**.

*SANT RAFEL DE FORCA

The small village of ***Sant Rafel de Forca ㉚** is only ten minutes by car from Eivissa and is reputed to be a hub of art and craftsmanship – of pottery in particular. Artists here offer wares of all kinds but also ceramics with Punic and Roman

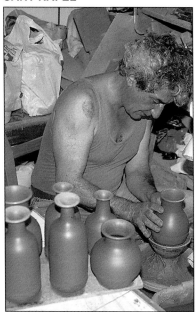

SANT RAFEL

motifs. Almost all the workshops are located in the village center and can be comfortably explored one by one. The artists always exhibit their work in front of their establishments and prices can be bargained.

A pretty little **fortress church** crowns the hill, from where there is a lovely view over the lowlands of Pla de Vila and Eivissa with its "city crown" – Dalt Vila. This vantage point is an absolute must for enthusiastic photographers. A 19th-century statue of Christ stands on a hill east of here and is a popular pilgrimage destination.

2.5 kilometers further north you'll get the chance to gamble part of your vacation budget on a trotting race in the **Hipódromo**. And slightly south of Sant Rafel you can indulge in nocturnal action. This is the home of the world-famous **Privilege** megadisco and another dance temple by the name of **Amnesia** which is famous for its wild foam parties.

Above: Pottery village Sant Rafel de Forca.

THE SOUTH AND WEST

ⓘ ⓢⓢⓢ **Victoria**, Ctra. St. Agustí, Cala Tirada, 3 km, tel. 608-340900, fax 342572; hotel which is open all year, spacious rooms on Comte Bay with a view of Isla Sa Conillera. ⓢⓢ **Tarida Beach**, Cala Tarida, tel. 608-800472; large hotel, cleverly-designed to blend in with the landscape, a covered path overgrown with blossoms leads down to the sandy bay. **Hacienda Cala Moli**, Cala Moli, tel. and fax 608-806002; small but stylish bungalow complex located right beside the sea. **Ses Pitreras**, Avda. Valladolid 1, Port des Torrent, tel. 971-345000, fax 346289; beautiful cubic building, well-equipped rooms, lots of regulars spend their winters here.

✕ **Carmen**, Cala d'Hort, Apt. 180, tel. 908-142661; specializing in seafood dishes and Ibizan paella which contains not only seafood but also chicken and rabbit. **Cas Mila**, Cala Tarida, tel. 608-800493; seafood restaurant located slightly above the beach, the *Guisado de Pescado* fish stew served here is extraordinarily delicious and you'll find halibut, red peppers, beans and potatoes simmering in it, live music is played on Saturdays during the peak season. **Es Boldadò**, Cala d'Hort, tel. 608-90883827; this restaurant is literally balanced on the northern cliff edge at the end of the bay, an exquisite *caldereta de langosta* (rock lobster soup) is available here. **Malibú**, Platja de ses Salines, tel. 608-305974; serves international cuisine and a wide range of seafood. **Can Jaume**, Platja Vadella, tel. 608-808127; Mediterranean cuisine, but above all paella, rice and seafood. **Rick's Café**, Carrer Valadolid 5, Port des Torrent, tel. 971-347654; sprawling establishment featuring a tropical garden, French cuisine. **Ay Jalisco**, situated along the old road from Port des Torrent, tel. 971-342393; Tex-Mex food.

🚢 *EXCURSIONS*: Boat trips to **Illa Es Vedrà**: From **Cala d'Hort**, **Cala Vedella** and **Cala Carbó**.

SANT JOSEP

🍸 **Bar Bernat Vinya**, Sant Josep de sa Talaia, Plaça de sa Església, tel. 971-340703; meeting place for both locals and tourists.

SANT AGUSTÍ D'ES VEDRÀ

✕ **Can Berri Vell**, Plaça de sa Església, tel. 971-344321; Spanish dishes served in what is presumably the oldest finca on the island – at least 500 years old.

🍸 **Bar Berri**, Plaça de sa Església; meeting place for the island's German-speaking community, beer and meatballs, open from 7 am in summer. **Naif**, PM 803, 3.9 km; open-air music bar with Ibizan-Arab touch, the DJ spins in one of the tents.

THE WEST

SANT ANTONI DE PORTMANY

 Oficina Municipal d'Informacio i Turisme (Tourist Information Office), Passeig de ses Fonts, tel. 971-343363.

 ⊙⊙⊙ Stella Maris, Cap Negret s/n, tel. 971-340600; Moorish-style club complex situated on a lush slope outside the town, good facilities for children. Pikes Hotel, Campo Ibiza (near Sant Antoni), tel. 971-342222, fax 342312, e-mail: pikes@ctv.es; modernized old finca where Julio Iglesias and Mick Jagger, plus their families, have stayed.

⊙⊙ Arenal, Avda. Dr. Fleming 16, tel. 971-340112, fax 342565; refurbished middle-class hotel right on the beach. Can Mirador, Apt. 209, tel. 971-345491, fax 345226; beautiful club establishment with pool, gym equipment, sauna and sweeping views of the archipelago, sea and the offshore islands to the southwest. Marco Polo, Avda. Portus Magnus s/n, tel. 971-341050; less sophisticated middle-class hotel at the town entrance, near the bay, swimming pool in its small park.

⊙ Mallorca, C/. de Mallorca 9, tel. 971-340161; simple but well-organized guest house located near the market hall.

🍴 Cafeteria es Clot, C/. Antonio Riquer; popular breakfast destination, slightly subdued atmosphere due to many people still being exhausted from the night before. Can Pujol, Ctra. Vella Port des Torrent s/n, tel. 971-341407; high-class fish restaurant, not exactly inexpensive. Rias Baixas, C/.d'Ignasi Riquer 4, tel. 971-340480; one of the best seafood restaurants on the whole island, located in an inconspicuous side street, Galician food. Sa Capella, Ctra. de Can Coix, 0.5 km, tel. 971-340057; restaurant in former chapel serving Spanish-Ibizan food with waiters dressed in traditional costume.

🍸 Café del Mar, C/. Lepanto 4, tel. 34 25 16; this is where the socialite jet set meets before taking off for the night; you can watch the sun sink behind the wide sea whilst enjoying the music here. Breakfast available from 9 am on. Es Paradis Terrenal, Avda. Dr. Fleming s/n; palms grow beneath its pyramid-shaped glass roofs, there are several dance floors, each featuring a different style of music, water games for cooling off, the finale takes place in a foam pool and the die-hards who stay until 6 am will be rewarded with a cooling group shower. Eden, Avda. Dr. Fleming, tel. 971-340737, large disco on two levels, very popular with young British tourists, foam party on Fridays. Extasis, at the entrance to Sant Antoni, in a hotel of the same name; teenagers are introduced to nocturnal rituals here, the more experienced offer a helping hand, at the end of the day (night) everybody has had a good time. Joe Spoon, C/. Santa Agnès 8; there is no closing hour in this Irish pub (with Guinness) and the atmosphere is always high-spirited. Night Life, C/. Santa Agnès 1, men have to pay an entrance charge, women get in free, the beer flows in rivers as this disco is firmly under British occupation. Play 2, C/. Santa Agnès 3; aged interior, but nevertheless always full to heaving, excellent atmosphere until the early hours.

Pussycat, Passeig Maritim, tel. 343064; everything here revolves around beer, some types are brewed according to the age-old German purity laws. Sgt. Pepper's, C/. del Mar 7; disco bar, occasionally featuring live bands, open daily, in fact it never closes.

📷 Cova Santa Agnès, can be reached on the road to Santa Agnès, on the right-hand side of which you'll see a signposted access road after about 2 km which will take you there. Only open Mon 9 am-noon and Sat 7-9 pm, the guided tour takes about 20 minutes.

📷 Quad Safari Through the hinterlands of Sant Antoni or along the coast by means of Quad Runner on four tough studded tyres (with or without driver). Rent a Quad, Avda. Dr. Fleming 38, tel. 971-342535.

SANTA AGNÈS DE CORONA

 ⊙⊙⊙ Can Pujolet, Agroturismo Santa Ines, Santa Ines (3 km north of Santa Agnès), tel. 971-805170, fax 805038, e-mail: ninac@mx3.redestb.es; converted former finca, superb location over valleys in an area dominated by almond trees, the eight apartments have been traditionally yet stylishly furnished, mountain bikes available.

🍴 Can Cosmi, at the church square, tel. 971-805020, open all year round; best tortilla espanola on the Pitiusas.

SANT RAFEL DE FORCA

🍴 C'an Bernat, Ctra. San Miquel, tel. 971-197014; beautifully-located establishment serving local cuisine. La Luna de Miel, on the main road, middle-class restaurant, well-frequented by the locals. L'Éléphant, Plaça des Esglesia, tel. 971-198056; serving French cuisine.

📷 Ceramicas Es Moli, Ceramicas Icardi and Ceramica Can Kinoto are the best-stocked workshops also selling their ceramic wares. They are all in the town center.

🍸 Privilege, on the road to Sant Antoni, 7 km (near Sant Rafel), tel. 971-198160; megadisco with space for up to 10,000 guest.

Amnesia, tel. 971-191041; large discotheque, on two levels, famous DJs spin their discs here, foam parties until 4 am.

South and west

THE NORTHEAST

THE NORTH
PORTINATX
THE EAST COAST
SANTA EULÀRIA
TALAMANCA

Northeast

There are no "fashionable" discos in the north, but between Portinatx and Port de Sant Miquel you'll be compensated with plenty of sheltered bays, picturesque cliffs, lush vegetation, pirate towers and mysterious caves.

Ibiza's eastern region is particularly family-friendly and holiday clubs here have adjusted themselves accordingly; from the touristic point of view the east coast beaches around Santa Eulària have an especially good infrastructure.

Santa Gertrudis de Fruitera

Along the road north, in the village of **Santa Gertrudis de Fruitera** ❶ in the hilly, fruit and vine-growing hinterlands, day-trippers will mostly meet the new, well-heeled islanders. At the weekends in particular, these "new residents" like to drive around in their smart cars or meticulously-polished motorbikes, sit in cafés, collect their mail, rummage around in antiques shops, lifestyle boutiques and galleries or cast an envious eye over the belongings of their competitors, all in a sophisticated swirl of cigar smoke.

This small village along the road north has only remained traditional around its 18th-century **church**. Contemporary ar-

Left: At S'Aigua Blanca's beach bar.

chitecture has sprung up on its outskirts. The cubic-style **Sa Nova Gertrudis** quarter didn't develop until the 1990s. Along its main road there is also an international bookshop called **Libro Azul** which is connected to a gallery. Ibicenco and foreign artists working on the island make a deliberate effort to exhibit in the renowned galleries of this town, as they are among the best sales platforms.

The owner of **Bar Costa**, where whole hams hang from the ceiling, is said to be the largest private collector on Ibiza. For years he accepted payment from needy artists in the form of paintings in exchange for drinks and food. In the meantime he hardly has any free space left on his walls. The artworks of several foreign artists he helped "feed," who have in the meantime acquired fame, have bestowed a considerable, belated fortune upon him.

Paintings, antiques and curiosities are entertainingly auctioned off ("3 fantastic white cement chickens – only 12,000 pesetas!") in the **Casi Todo** auction house.

The **Galeria es Moli** on the road to Sant Miquel proves that with a lot of courage one art lover was able to reach the rank of top art dealer on the island. Here, local and international artists are displayed by the French owner, including Dalí, Miró and Picasso (only open in the evenings).

THE NORTH

Sant Miquel de Balansat

Sant Miquel de Balansat ❷ is located in the green northern part of the island, right in the middle of the agricultural region. Its houses are clustered around the imposing fortress church of **★Sant Miquel Arcangel** which was erected on a hill in the 16th century and is dedicated to the archangel Michael. The side of the church facing the road appears inviting with its round arches, but the back of it presents itself as a bulwark. The main nave with Gothic arches, together with both side chapels, constitutes a cruciform. The ceiling and wall paintings of the **Capella de Benirrás**, extended in 1691, are worth seeing; it was restored in

Above: Needy artists used to be able to pay their tab in Bar Costa in Santa Gertrudis with their artworks. Right: Swimming in the sheltered bay of Port de Sant Miquel is a pleasure all year round.

1994 by international specialists. The arch through which one enters the church carries the name *Porta de Ses Dones* or "women's gate." A vast and popular **★folklore festival** with Ibizan music, traditional costume-dancing and local wine-tasting, as well as an arts and crafts market takes place on Thursday evenings in the forecourt of the parish church.

Today Sant Miquel distinguishes itself as the small hub of the north and profits from this in its touristic harbor town of Port de Sant Miquel, 4 kilometers away.

Port de Sant Miquel

During the days of the initial tourist boom the once-idyllic bay of **Port de Sant Miquel ❸**, already popular in antiquity as a natural, sheltered harbor, was developed into the perfect resort. However, it does give a somewhat sterile impression, as do all towns with mass accommodation. The largest hotels were built into the slope. Port de Sant Miquel has many souvenir shops, restaurants, bars and one

Northeast

small discotheque. The entire bay is sheltered from the wind, meaning that one can also swim here outside the main tourist season. A hiking path along the western side of the bay will bring you to the small bay of **Cala dels Moltons** and the ruins of the historic **Torre d'Es Molar** fortress tower.

Located slightly further northeast and very popular with sailors the sand bay of ***Cala de Benirrás**, with its beguiling crystal-clear waters, is a meeting point for hippies on Sundays and full moon nights who sit here making music or just drumming into the early hours.

*Cova de Can Marçá

*Cova de Can Marçá, located northeast of Port de Sant Miquel near Platja de Sant Miquel, was famous as a "smugglers' hideaway" in the old days. People who carried out their business on the other side of the law found a natural depot for their wares here. Experts have unearthed the fossils and bones of long-

extinct animals, above all very large birds, but also the red and black markings that guided the smugglers to their escape routes. This spacious cave is estimated to be over 1,000 years old. The old passages appear enchanted, the limestone pillars have surely witnessed a thousand secrets and the stalactite formations are, by any accounts, bizarre. Water trickling from above combines with dissolved limestone and gives rise to an ideal environment for stalactite (from the ceiling) and stalagmite (on the floor) formations. Guided tours include colorful light shows accompanied by music and a computer-controlled waterfall which cascades down the rocks. After the show the water is pumped back up again. (Open daily from 10:30 am-1:30 pm and 3-7 pm.)

*Na Xamena

The beautiful bay of ***Na Xamena ❹** is crowned by the **La Hacienda** hotel – until now the only five-star hotel on the Pitiusas. Its interior decoration and above

all its "historical cuisine" is a revival of Punic times, one of the island's oldest and longest historical chapters. Its restaurant successfully demonstrates that the Carthaginians possessed a highly-sophisticated sense of the culinary; old recipes are copied and adapted to suit the expectations of modern taste buds.

Below the hotel's charming pool area is a small beach – one of the most beautiful on the island – to which you can descend on foot, albeit with some difficulty. But it is better reached by boat, from where you can get a fine view of this impressive cliff setting.

*Sant Llorenç de Balàfia

The time-honored village of ***Sant Llorenç de Balàfia ❺** gives a pretty and well-maintained impression. The earth

Above: The people of the village of Balàfia always found a safe refuge in their impenetrable defense towers. Right: An ancient olive tree near Sant Joan de Labritja.

displays a strong red hue here, contrasting the lush green of the pastureland. The layers of stone walls contributing to arable terracing have been carefully constructed; sheep graze beneath the ancient olive trees around the *fincas*.

Quite unlike Santa Gertrudis, Sant Llorenç has managed to retain its original appearance. This tiny village of scattered houses, farmsteads and an 18th-century parish **church** is located approximately 10 kilometers from the sea in the fertile **Es Pla d'Atzaró** plain. This was always a fairly wealthy settlement, which is why it always had to defend itself against the attacks of pirates and other malevolent contemporaries.

For the same reason a truly defensive style of architecture came into being in the hamlet of ****Balàfia** further northeast. The French architect Le Corbusier referred to it as "peculiar and pure architecture." Before the maritime criminals could advance the inhabitants would ascend their three **defense towers** by means of rope ladders. The towers had no

accessways from below and when the rope ladders were pulled up the tower's occupiers remained untouchable. They did, however, have to wait until the air was clear again before descending. These quarrystone towers were once painted with white crosses to ward off evil spirits. Next to them you'll see cubic, Moorish-style farmhouses. In keeping with the traditional style of architecture on the island the residents here have lined the entrances to their houses with natural stone. Phoenician juniper trees, known as *sabinas* in these parts, used to form the gateways to the gardens and stables.

Despite being a tourist you'll experience surprisingly close encounters with the archetypal lifestyle of this region. This also applies to the food served in the rustic country hotel **Es Pins**, east beyond Sant Llorenç: the cuisine here is authentic and includes *sofrit pagès* – a nutritious stew – and also a special kind of *paella*. Brown, stone-oven baked bread and local home-made wines provide the perfect accompaniment for these dishes.

PORTINATX

Portinatx ❻ is one of the island's more modern villages: well-developed but unspectacular. The British first introduced it to tourism and they still represent the largest contingent of foreign visitors.

The village is surrounded by some of Ibiza's most beautiful bays. The three beaches of **Petit Arenal**, shaded by tall pines, **Grand Arenal**, enlarged thanks to more sand and also equipped with a water slide, as well as the narrow ***Cala Es Port**, the sand beach of which cuts deeply into the bay, all belong to the village of Portinatx. Small boats drop anchor here and there are a few modest restaurants.

Just before the harbor a sign directs you to ***Cala Xarraca** ❼ which is also a beach enlarged by the hand of man and which is considered especially romantic by both couples and solitary travelers alike. The sprawling villa on the hill overlooking it once belonged to the actress Ursula Andress (1962 Bond girl in *Dr. No*).

East of Portinatx the **Cala d'En Serra** presents itself as a quiet alternative to the busier beaches.

Sant Joan de Labritja

Sant Joan ❽ is a community of only 4,000 souls. It is a kind of cultural reserve for hippies and is possessed by a liberal spirit; esoterics and former disciples of Bhagwan flock here.

The inhabitants of Sant Joan are an efficient and pragmatic people who love to beautify their little village. This place really is one of the prettiest communities on the island and it is engulfed by vineyards, potato fields and meadows full of almond and carob trees. In addition to its beauty it is also the administrative seat of the little hamlets of Balansat, Balàfia, Portinatx and Sa Cala. Even the old veterans of that famous flower power subculture have devoted their services to this stunning town. They all live in well-maintained houses, some of the bars and stores are managed by them, but non-medical practitioners and fortune-tellers also have the opportunity to make a good living here.

The hub of the alternative scene here has always been **Bar Vista Alegre** where superb wine straight from the barrel, home-made herb liqueur (*hierbas*) and delicious island specialties are served. You'll find this bar beside the 18th-century **Església de Sant Joan** church.

An early morning hike north to Portinatx and the sea (3 hours) or to **★Furnas** hill, a 410-meter-high observation point south of Sant Joan in the **Serra de la Mala Costa**, is highly recommended and takes about two hours.

THE EAST COAST

Sant Vicenç

The quiet, scattered settlement of **Sant Vicenç de sa Cala ❾** is extremely pretty and very secluded in its pirate-proof loca-

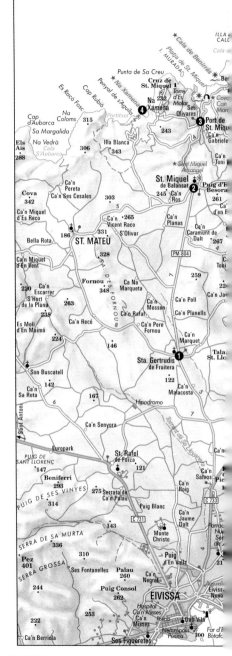

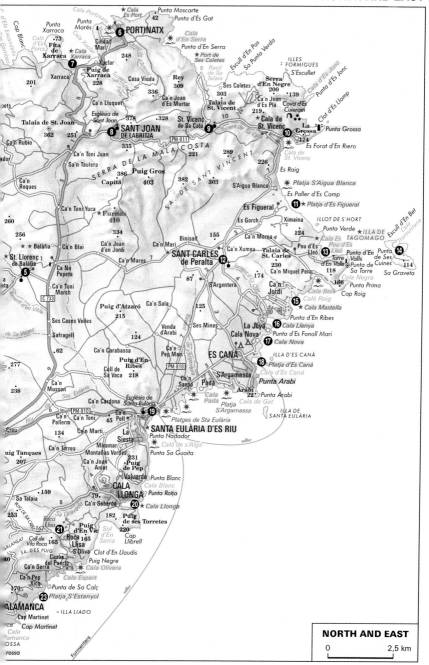

Northeast

tion, 3 kilometers from the coast in the rolling hinterlands. The town's white **church** used to serve as the perfect refuge: when attacks were imminent the people from the surrounding area would hide here. This simple vaulted church was completed in 1771 and has several chapels with classicistic altars and statues of saints. The statue of Saint Jacob with a scallop is of particular value.

A bar and a shop selling all kinds of odds and ends are both in close proximity to the church.

You'll can hike 6 kilometers eastward to the bay of Sant Vicenç by following the falcon-marked hiking route. An especially attractive detour leads northward to the pretty pebble bay of ***Port de Ses Caletes**.

Above: On Saturdays one can purchase local, organically-grown produce at Mercado del Campo (Can Sort, near Sant Joan). Right: The sand beach of Es Figueral with the club resort of Cala Blanca – very popular in the summer months.

*Cala de Sant Vicenç

The resort of ***Cala de Sant Vicenç** ⑩ is framed by tree-covered slopes. This promontory jutting prettily out to sea ends at **Punta Grossa**; a magnificent view of the coastline can be enjoyed from the hill of **La Grossa** (174 meters). In 1907 in the **Cova d'Es Cuieram**, a nearby cave, archaeologists discovered the famous bust of the Punic goddess, Tanit. The beautiful little bay of **Cala d'Es Jonc**, a little further north, can only be reached on foot or by boat.

Even though Cala de Sant Vicenç itself is crammed full of hotels of the larger variety, its sand beach is wide, its waters are clear and the bay itself is sheltered. Deckchair, sunshade and pedal boat rentals provide for a good living here. Young people are the exception rather than the rule in this place, as the residents of the town are somewhat cut off from the "pleasure boat" of Eivissa; bus connections aren't so good here and taxis are expensive due to the distance. Which suits

Northeast

the sun-worshippers and peace-loving vacationers here just fine, as they prefer to keep to themselves in this beautiful *cala*.

Es Figueral

The resort of **Es Figueral** ⓫ with its 1970's constructions couldn't possibly be described as charming, but its asset is that it is connected to ***Platja d'es Figueral,** a wide beach of dark sand in a stunning location framed by offshore rocks. The club complex of **Cala Blanca,** located just above the beach, encompasses restaurants, shops and a supermarket and is under the firm control of Germans. Diving and windsurfing schools offer their services and there is a specially-allocated area for beachball.

The long, narrow, sand beach of **S'Aigua Blanca** (*Aigües Blanques*) – the region's official naturist beach – lies further to the north and is intermittently punctuated by cliffs. It is well-frequented not only by veteran hippies but also by families with children.

*Sant Carles de Peralta

The small through-town of ***Sant Carles** ⓬ is a commercial center for the region's hippies and their descendants. In **Las Dalias**, 1 kilometer west of Sant Carles, flower children offer their products for sale at the local ***hippie market**. Many of them are skilled craftspeople and make and sell everything from jewelry or pottery to woven rugs and Bali-style sarongs. Deals between these original veterans of the woodstock generation are still generally sealed by a friendly handshake.

Anita's Bar serves as a sort of news desk, a hub of communication and high spirits where the hippies can also pick up their mail. The bar is a post office where you can enjoy a drink amid post office boxes while trying to make sense of what your relatives are reporting to you. In addition to the bar there is one more shop, a fortress-like 18th-century **village church** with a crucifixion scene and the **Sa Peralta** tourist restaurant.

**The Coast between Punta d'en Valls and Punta Arabí

There are some wildly-romantic bays east of Sant Carles just waiting to be discovered, for example the *Cala es Pou d'es Lleó ⑬ which is ideal for snorkeling. One of the best-preserved pirate towers, the **Torre d'en Valls**, still stands tall on the **Punta des Valls** cape from where you can enjoy a beautiful, sweeping view out over the uninhabited island of Tagomago.

The craggy island of *Illa de Tagomago ⑭ used to be the territory of only a handful of fishermen. The fact that a German was allowed to open a restaurant on this nature reserve outraged a lot of Ibicencos. The establishment of a resort on this small island was successfully blocked by a civic action group. It's very

Above: At the hippie market of Las Dalias near Sant Carles de Peralta. Right: The Puig de Missa is crowned by the fortress-like church of Església de Santa Eulària.

easy to reach the island by boat from Santa Eulària; it is only 1.5 km² in area, 114 meters high and is a major nesting ground for gulls. Divers and snorkelers will be rewarded with interesting underwater scenery all around this rocky little island.

The dark sand beach of **Cala Boix**, which can only be reached by means of a flight of steps, has hardly been developed at all. The small, neighboring fishing bay of *Cala Mastella ⑮ is home to a nice beach which has been topped up with extra sand. This is where you can find "the real McCoy" – an authentic mustached specimen by the name of *Don Bigotes* who runs a seafood restaurant. It is probably the most original fish restaurant on the Pitiusas and can only be reached by means of a forest path from Can Jordi. Advance reservation is essential; there is no telephone. There is also no menu to speak of, you eat what is put in front of you. Usually it's fish soup cooked in a cauldron over an open fire and a well-seasoned *guisado de pescado-arroz*. This is

accompanied by rice cooked in fish broth, considered by most guests to be the best part of the meal, and *porrón*, the house wine, served from a long-necked bottle.

The 100-meter-wide **Cala Llenya** 🔟 is located on the wide estuary of a dried-up stream. The bay is enclosed on both sides by rocks and its sand is very finely-grained. The sea bed subsides very gradually so it is perfectly safe for children to play and swim here. There is one restaurant and one boat rental agency. There are also some beautiful walks inland from here.

The **Cala Nova** 🔟 is a coarsely-grained, natural sand beach split by rocks in its center. **La Joya**, a large apartment complex, extends alongside it.

The large beach of **Platja d'es Caná** 🔟 (*Es Canyar*) is encircled by hotels and holiday houses and is a fairly lively spot due to the bus route connecting it to Santa Eulària which hauls in fresh holidaymakers daily. The sand beach is very pleasant and suitable for families, and the bay is very calm.

A sprawling **hippie market** takes place every Wednesday on the grounds of the nearby **Club Punta Arabi**.

The sand bay of **Cala Pada**, with a club hotel and boat rental facilities, is very popular and suitable for children. It is only a 3-minute walk from Santa Eulària.

*SANTA EULÀRIA D'ES RIU

The small town of ***Santa Eulària d'es Riu** 🔟 is the smallest of the 3 main resorts on the island. It has the longest sand beach and a relaxed atmosphere, but without the busy nightlife.

The British, along with their beer and fish'n'chip culture, were among the first imports of tourism. But the Ibicencos couldn't relate and have in the meantime taken charge of their own old, rustic restaurants again and the Spanish tapas culture here has successfully made up for all that lost time. Even the raging hotel building boom which defaced the town in the 1970s has been steered back on a more acceptable course. The well-maintained **Platja,** which has been reinforced with extra sand, extends from the **marina** ❶ with its elegant yachts and restaurants (outstanding: *Doña Margarita*) as far as the Riu estuary at Mariners Beach. The **Passeig Maritim** ❷, a palm-lined, spacious harbor promenade running parallel to the beach, is very inviting for a stroll. There are innumerable modern cafés, ice-cream kiosks (*Miretti* serves excellent gelato) and restaurants with tables outside.

The shady ***Rambla** ❸ (*Passeig de S'Alamara*), a short pedestrian zone between the beach promenade and the Sant Jaume main road, constitutes the focal point of the town. Souvenir dealers, portrait painters and street artists all carry out their business here. The monument at the top end of the palm-fringed **Plaça d'Espanya** ❹, which is also the site of the town hall, is dedicated to the town's seafarers who saved the distressed passengers and crew of the SS *Mallorca* in 1930. This is also the departure point for a two-hour sightseeing trip on a rubber-tyred tram.

Busy **Carrer Sant Jaume** divides the town into two halves: the new quarter and the historic upper town. In the "fashionable quarter" of town around ***Carrer Sant Vicent** ❺ you'll find lots of chic boutiques and good restaurants; in the evening it mutates into a pedestrianized "eating zone." During the daytime you can shop in the modern **Mercat** ❻ market hall along Carrer del Sol, where you can stock up on fruit, vegetables and delicious *tapas.*

The **old town** is characterized by white cubic houses and is one of the most beautiful sights on Ibiza. It is located at the foot of the 66-meter-high **Puig de Missa** hill, where the whitewashed fortress church of ****Església de Santa Eulària** ❼, which has a mighty defense tower, stands defiant under the burning sun. It was constructed in the 14th century over the foundations of an Arab mosque. This hill wasn't always the peaceful place it

appears today: the small town was often the point of attack for marauding pirates. To put a decisive end to this constant threat the church was built with walls several meters thick, resulting in what is probably the most striking fortress church on the Pitiusas. Until the early 20th century there were cannons on its rooftop.

The neighboring **Cementeri des Puig de Missa** is a cemetery where the dead were laid to rest above the ground – in mortuaries up to five storeys high. Residents even include Germans, British, Dutch and Italians.

The historic farmhouse of Can Ros was transformed into an ethnological museum (**Museu Etnològic**) which exhibits traditional old folk costumes, kitchen implements, tools and a wine cellar.

There is an entertaining legend about the **old bridge** ❽ over the river *Riu*: when the original footbridge was destroyed by the swollen river for the umpteenth time the mayor decided that was the last straw. "Let the devil rebuild it!" he angrily shouted. No sooner were his words spoken than the devil turned up and promised the mayor he would have the bridge rebuilt before the next day dawned. As quid pro quo he wanted the living soul of the first being to cross the new bridge. The mayor agreed. The next morning the townspeople couldn't believe their eyes – the bridge really was rebuilt, but nobody wanted to be the first to cross it. The mayor resorted to a cunning trick and shooed a dog across. The devil was outraged and in his anger tore several stones from the structure, then disappeared. In truth, there really are a few stones missing from the old bridge. Nowadays it is only used by pedestrians. But over time the bridge almost lost the water beneath it: the river is the only one to flow naturally all year long and it was the river that drove the old corn mills and helped make the city affluent, but the very high water consumption of all the hotels is a significant factor in the low water level.

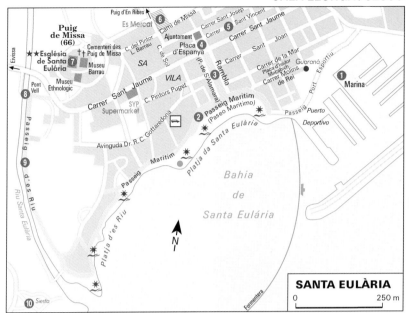

Northeast

SANTA EULÀRIA
0   250 m

Walking along the palm-fringed **Passeig d'es Riu** ❾ river bed toward the sea via a wooden bridge over the Riu estuary you'll reach the resort of **Siesta** ❿ with its many white villas. Alternatively, if you walk 2 kilometers in a northwesterly direction from the new town you'll come to the 218-meter lookout hill of **Puig d'En Ribes.**

*Cala Llonga

The fjord-like bay of *Cala Llonga ⓴ (4 kilometers south of Santa Eulària) shimmers a deep shade of blue and has a 200-meter beach of fine sand. It is ideal for families with children and perfect for building sand castles. The flat bay is framed by hotels and cliffs and opens out to the east; a forest stream enters the sea here. In addition to the many restaurants and bars there are plenty of water sports facilities. Visitors walking toward **Punta Rotja** will be rewarded with an exceptionally fine view of cliffs, green pine forests and the luminescent sea.

There are two small swimming bays near the **Roca Llisa Golf Club** ㉑ (27-hole course, open to all): craggy **Cala Olivera**, a mere 30 meters wide, and the narrow bay of **Cala Espart**.

Jesús

Jesús ㉒ is home to Ibiza's most beautiful altar. It is located in a modest fortress church dating back to 1549, slightly out-of-the-way between walls and gardens. The **Parroquia de Nuestra Senora de Jesús** was completely restored in 1992 and since then the Gothic **altarpiece, in seven sections, has reclaimed its fame as a pilgrimage site for art lovers. It is designed in the style of the Valencian school and its creator was *Juan Rodrigo de Osona*. The scenes from the Life of Mary and the Apostle are absolute must-sees.

We recommend an excursion 4 kilometers east from Jesús. It will take you along a bumpy road to the 100-meter-wide beach of **Platja s'Estanyol** ㉓ with coarse sand and a beach bar.

★Talamanca

★Talamanca ❷ is now a suburb of Eivissa, yet it possesses its very own flair and atmosphere. The two towns are separated by the cape of **Punta Grossa** whose sweeping bay is home to a wide beach of finely-grained sand, making it excellent territory for swimmers, windsurfers and sun-worshippers. It is much more peaceful here than on the beaches southwest of the capital, which are under the airport's approach corridor, and children will be enraptured by the aquatic park of **Agualandia** which has some thrilling water slides.

Since the 1960s some architecturally-ambitious villas have mushroomed in the hills surrounding **Cap Martinet**, slightly further to the east, and they are well worth seeing.

Above: The late-Gothic altarpiece (section) dating back to 1598 in the Parraquia de Nuestra Senora de Jesús church is a sight worth seeing for art aficionados.

THE NORTH

SANTA GERTRUDIS DE FRUITERA
🛏 😊😊 **Cas Gasi**, Apto. 117, tel. and fax 971-197173, e-mail: casgasi@steinweb.net; agro-tourism in what was once a finca, now re-styled into a refuge of luxury.

❌ **Bar Costa**, tel. 971-197021; legendary restaurant with art on the walls and hams hanging from the ceiling; paella in enormous pans. **Amar Lu**, along the country road to Eivissa, tel. 971-314554; Basque cuisine.

🍴 **Geranio Rosa**, Banca Matutes 2, tel. 971-197053; family-run business with international cuisine and a comfortable bar. **La Plaza**, Plaça d'es Esglesia, tel. 971-197075; refined restaurant with a palm garden, French cuisine. **Ca'n Cans**, C 804, 3.5 km, tel. 971-197516; country-style restaurant with specialties from the grill.

🍴 **Casi Todo**, tel. 971-197023, furniture, paintings and curios, open daily 11 am-8 pm except Sundays, auctions on first Saturday of every month in summer:

SANT MIQUEL DE BALANSAT
🛏 😊😊 **C'as Ola**, Aptdo. Correos 777, tel. 971-334587, fax 334604; new hotel in old surroundings.

❌ **Can Gall**, Ctra. de Sant Joan, 11.6 km (near Sant Llorenc), tel. 971-332916; renowned for its delicious grilled meats.

Cana Pepeta, Ctra. de Sant Joan, 14.4 km, tel. 971-631949; traditional Ibizan cuisine.

Es Caliu, Ctra. de Sant Joan, 10.8 km, tel. 971-325072; local and international dishes.

PORT DE SANT MIQUEL
🛏 😊😊 **Cartago**, Port de Sant Miquel, tel. 971-334551; middle-class hotel.

NA XAMENA
🛏 😊😊😊 **Hacienda**, Na Xamena, tel. 971-334500, fax 334606, www.relaischateau.fr-xamena; only luxury hotel on the Pitiusas, beautiful location on a steep cliff, every room has a sea view, tasteful furnishings, own beach.

❌ **Las Cascadas Suenos de Oro**, in the Na Xamena Hotel, Urb. San Juan Bautista, tel. 971-334500; Ibizan, Spanish and international specialties.

PORTINATX
🛏 😊😊 **Club Hotel Portinatx**, tel. 971-320540, overlooking the small bay of Cala S'Imatge; all-inclusive club on a slope, spacious gardens, 3 tennis courts, sailing instruction.

SANT JOAN DE LABRITJA

🛏 😊😊 **Can Marti**, tel. 971-333500, fax 333112; agrotourism.

❌ **Bar Vista Alegre**, near the church, tel. 971-333008; hangout for long-serving hippies, delicious snacks.

🛍 **Eco,** Plaça de Espanya 5, tel. 971-333029, e-mail dspiegel@infonegocio.com; New Age store with health food, cosmetics and all kinds of odds and ends; e-mail service.

THE EAST

ES FIGUERAL

🛏 😊😊 **Cala Blanca**, Playa d'es Figueral, tel. 971-335100/01, fax 335040; large complex in a sandy bay.

❌ **Es Caló**, Platja Cala Sant Vicenç, tel. 971-320140; Mediterranean cuisine.

SANT CARLES DE PERALTA

🛏 😊😊😊 **Can Curreu**, Ctra. Sant Carles, 12 km, tel. and fax 971-335280; one of the most beautifully-converted fincas, several houses on the slope with majestic views, open all year round. 😊😊 **Can Talaias**, Sant Carles, tel. 971-335742, fax 331161; agro-tourism in a former finca.

❌ **Las Dalias,** Ctra. Sant Carles, 12 km, tel. 971-330742; local and international cuisine. **Anita's Bar**, near the church, tel. 971-335090; good tapas.

TAGOMAGO ISLAND

🛍 Boats run from the harbor in **Santa Eulària** to the island of **Tagomago**. You can also rent a boat and cross over yourself. **Rent-a-boat**, Puerto Deportivo, cellphone 610-217291.

SANTA EULÀRIA D'ES RIU

ℹ️ **Oficina Municipal de Información**, Carrer Mariano Riquer Wallis 4, tel. 971-330728.

🛏 😊😊😊 **Sa Colina**, C 733, 1 km outside town, tel. and fax 971-332767; former finca converted into a country hotel by Swiss people, rustic, comfortable, but at the same time sophisticated. **Les Terrasses**, C 733, 1 km outside town, tel. 971-332643, fax 338978; mini-hotel with exclusive decor, on the mountain, lovely views – even from the pool. 😊😊 **Ca's Catala**, Carrer del Sol s/n, tel. 971-331006, fax 339268; pretty little house in town, garden with pool, friendly atmosphere. **La Cala**, Carrer Huesca 1, tel. 971-330009, fax 331512; hotel with pool close to the beach, but only a few of the rooms have sea views. **Sol Club S'Argamassa**, Urb. S'Argamassa, tel. 971-330051, fax 330076; club hotel in Cala Martina bay outside of town. **Sol Familia Loros**, Finca C'as Capitá s/n, tel. 971-330761, fax 339542;

large hotel with almost 300 rooms and family-friendly facilities in a quiet area near the yacht harbor. 😊 **Sa Rota**, Carrer Sant Vicent 89, tel. and fax 971-330022; well-organized *hostal*.

❌ **Dona Margarita**, Puerto Deportivo, tel. 971-332200; gourmet seafood restaurant which has even received a few awards. **Rincon de Pepe**, Carrer Sant Vicent 53, tel. 971-331321; tapas bar, very traditional, with a beautiful patio. **Can Miquel,** Carrer Sant Vicent 43, tel. 971-330329; fish restaurant with a wide range of choice. **Bahia Santa Eulària**, Carrer Molins de Rey s/n, tel. 971-330828; promenade restaurant with terrace and Spanish cuisine. **Royalty**, Carrer Sant Jaume 51, tel. 971-331819; café-restaurant in central location on Plaça d'Espanya.

El Bigote, popular, traditional seafood restaurant in Cala Mastella, no telephone. Can be reached via the road from San Carles to Can Jordi – the way is signposted. Reservations essential: either personally or through: http://www.global-spirit.com/Ibiza.

🍸 **Taberna Andaluza**, Carrer Sant Vicent 51, tel. 971-336772; delicious *tapas*. **Studio 64**, Carrer Sant Joan, corner of Carr. Sant Llorenc; disco, no age restrictions. **Top Hat**, Plaça d'Isidoro Macabich; nightclub.

🛍 **Ibiza Diving**, Puerto Deportivo, tel. 971-332949, fax 332899; paragliding, **Centro Deportivo Nautico Boca Rio**, Sa Feixa Baixa s/n, tel. 971-331984. **Bicycle Rental Kandani**, road to Es Canyar 109, tel. 971-339264.

CALA LLONGA

🛏 😊😊 **Playa Imperial**, tel. 971-196471, fax 196491, hotel resort overlooking the sea.

❌ **Grill Sa Font**, tel. 971-196269; garden restaurant on the beach, fish dishes and paella.

🛍 **Dive Center Rumbo Azul**, tel. 971-348242, diving in this bay is hard to resist, good introductory offers available for beginners.

🏌 **Club de Golf Ibiza/Club de Golf Roca Lisa**, on the road from Jesús to Cala Llonga, tel. 971-196052, fax 196051; open all year.

JESÚS

🛏 😊😊 **Casa Alexio**, Barrio ses Torres 16, tel. 971-314249, fax 312619; open all year, modern, with pool and air-conditioning, very popular with gay people.

TALAMANCA

🛏 😊😊😊 **El Corso**, Platja Talamanca s/n, tel. 971-312312, fax 312703; best establishment in Talamanca, with pool and view of Dalt Vila. 😊 **Hostal Talamanca**, Platja Talamanca s/n, tel. 971-312463, fax 315716; basic, but right on the beach.

Northeast

FORMENTERA

**FORMENTERA

Formentera is mostly flat and small enough (23 kilometers long and 1.5 kilometers wide in parts) to cycle across in only one day whilst enjoying the surrounding natural beauty: cypress junipers (*sabina marítima*), carob trees, pine, fig and olive trees, opuntias and agaves, macchia of white rockrose, rosemary and thyme, karstic pastureland dotted with goats and long, sandy beaches punctuated by rocks. Cyclists will only work up a sweat when they attempt the picturesque ascent to the plateau of La Mola at 192 meters.

History

The smallest of the Balearic Islands is sparsely populated (approx. 6,000 inhabitants, 1,000 of them foreigners) yet makes a point of retaining its own identity so as not to be passed off as a mere appendage of Ibiza. This island has its own history, of which its residents are very proud: Formentera was already settled 3,800 years ago, as verified by the megalithic tomb of Ca Na Costa near Es Pujols. Finds from the early Stone Age were discovered in several locations. Little remains to remind us of the long Punic Era (654-123 B.C.), but an abundance of Roman remnants are still visible today, like the Roman road between Es Caló and La Mola, the Roman camp of Castell Romà and, above all, the island's name: it is said to have been derived from the Latin *frumentaria* (rich in cereals) and even today wheat and oats are successfully cultivated on this parched limestone island. The Moors also left their legacy here from the 10th century A.D.; terraces, fountains and irrigation canals remind us of their advanced agricultural know-how.

After Catalan King James I expelled the Muslims in 1235 Formentera was largely ignored by its new Aragon rulers, rendering it defenseless against the terrifying Berber pirates of North Africa based a mere 250 nautical miles from its shores. In the 15th century the population collectively packed up, cleared off the island and resettled on Ibiza. The only people left on Formentera were the guards stationed in the old Saracen watchtowers who would warn the Ibicencos if pirates were at large. Formentera remained deserted for almost two centuries. Toward the end of the 17th century the first settlers ventured back and made their living through agricultural means and salt extraction. They established Sant Francesc

Left: Fiesta with folk-dancing events in Sant Ferran.

Formentera

in 1726; since then, the island has never again been deserted.

Compared with Ibiza the rhythm of these natives is relaxed and life takes a comfortable, stress-free course – a fact much appreciated by those who have flown modern civilization to resettle here. Between September and June peace-loving individualists will be in their element on this island.

Fifty years ago there wasn't a single hotel here. Now though, as 150,000 sun-starved souls are kindly accommodated annually, the islanders tend to deal with their guests at a dignified distance.

It was artists who first discovered the rough charm of the island in the 1950s and the first hippies had settled here by the 1960s. The Formenteranos with their tanned skin, sturdy necks, calloused fishermen's hands and calm temperament watched on in amazement as the flower

Above: The beach of Cavall d'En Borrás (near Cala Savina) can be easily reached by moped or bicycle.

children stepped out of their clothes on the beaches, cavorted about in the waves in the altogether, made love on the sand, drank sangria and crooned their psychedelic anthems at night accompanied by guitars and bongos in the light of their flickering candles and enshrouded in a mist of sweet-smelling hash fumes. Neither resistance nor bonding took place; both sides remained in their own world.

*La Savina

The ferries from Ibiza, the fastest of which (express boats) cross the Es Freus straits in only 30 minutes, dock at the harbor of *La Savina ❶ which was named after the Phoenician juniper tree. All visitors arrive here, as there is no airport. The island's only harbor was recently extended with a new yacht *marina. Yet the old fishermen still sit here mending their nets as they have always done. Restaurants, hostals and shops are open for business; car, motorbike and bicycle rentals display their offers.

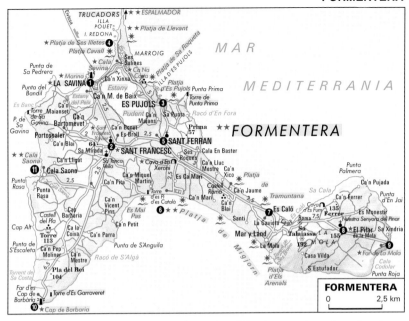

Formentera boasts the highest density of rental bikes on the planet, but it must be said that these are usually automatically included in package deals. There is a scheduled bus service along the island's main road to La Mola. You can take a walk along the harbor mole and rest in one of the bars to take in the atmosphere, for example in the attractive **Gecko's Café**.

In the west the town borders on **Estany del Peix**, a fishing hub in antiquity, and in the east on the brackish water lagoon of **Estany Pudent**, formerly connected to the salinas and which can smell a little unpleasant in summertime. Also located in the east is the white, pine-lined, sandy beach of **★Cala Savina** and **Platja Cavall**.

★Sant Francesc de Formentera

★Sant Francesc ❷ (1,500 residents) is the island's administrative capital and the mayor and police form the state authority; its only prison cell is usually empty. A lot of development has taken place in recent years and a pedestrian zone has also been created. In addition to the obligatory souvenir and handicrafts shops, galleries, banks, stores and good restaurants, like the **Fonda Plate** for example, there is also a folk museum or **★Museu Etnològic** which exhibits an old salt-mining locomotive in its yard. Both locals and visitors like to meet up at the paved church square – the **Plaça de sa Constitucio** – lined by palm and olive trees. The comfortable **Café Centro** is a popular venue on this square.

The church of **★Sant Francesc Xavier** with walls three meters thick wasn't built until 1726 after the island was resettled. It used to have cannons on its roof for keeping pirates at bay. By contrast, the **Capella sa Tanca Vella** south of town was built in the 14th century during the Catalan period.

A wholesome country loaf of cereals grown on Formentera is made in the **Geroni** bakery in Sant Francesc, as well as delicious cakes.

Es Pujols

Originally just a bay with a few boat shelters the settlement of **Es Pujols** ❸ has mutated into a tourist hub. It has been very well designed and its layout is easy to grasp; everything is easily accessible on foot. Sprawling hotels were never built here, although they had originally been planned.

Nowadays this former fishing village is fully equipped to meet the needs of the modern-day beach tourist, thanks to the long sand beach of **Platja d'Es Pujols,** which is also very popular with windsurfers, and the smaller beach of **Platja de Sa Roqueta**.

Its infrastructure is very much tourist-oriented and there is even a disco, the **Tipíc**. The strolling zone of **Passeig de Miramar** is home to several open-air

Above: The fortress-like church of Sant Francesc Xavier. Right: Richly-colored illuminations in Cova d'En Xeroni.

bars as well as a handicrafts market which takes place in the evenings in front of the Sa Volta hotel.

Club Punta Prima, located on the cape, was specially designed to blend in with the landscape. The **Torre de Punta Prima** – Formentera's best-preserved fortress tower – looms up over the entire area and the **La Gavina** restaurant serves superb Balearic cuisine.

Just 1 kilometer northwest a well-signposted road leads to the 4,000-year-old megalithic tomb of ★**Ca Na Costa**. The site was unearthed by archaeologists in 1974 and had to be subsequently fenced off to deter "souvenir collectors." Since then this invaluable discovery has been roofed over. Stone tools and the skeletons of both men and women were found at this site.

★★Platja de Llevant and ★Platja de Ses Illetes

Continuing northward past the **salinas** (now a nature conservation area), which were once extremely important to the island's economy, you reach **Trucadors** – the sandy northern edge of the island with the popular dune beaches of ****Platja de Llevant** and ***Platja de Ses Illetes** ❹ (for naturists), 3 kilometers long. This is also the home of the famous seafood restaurant **Es Moli del Sal** in an old salt mill – a favorite venue among skippers – and the beach restaurant of **Juan y Andrea**.

If you wade 200 meters from the northern tip you'll reach the mini-islet of ****Espalmador** which has many lovely sand bays and even offers the opportunity of bathing in mud.

Sant Ferran

The living legend (in bar terms) of **Sant Ferran** ❺ (*San Fernando*, approx. 1,000 residents) is the ***Fonda Pepe** bar beside the simple quarrystone church. It still carries the name of its owner, who built it with his own hands in 1953; he passed away in 1995. This world-famous bar is the shrine and nucleus of the flower power movement on the Balearics; it originated as a simple village pub with a dark bar, but today also has a restaurant and rents out rooms. "To see and be seen" has been a pastime here since the 1960s, but you can also eat well, e.g. delicious leg of lamb. At some point every visitor to Formentera will drop in here for a drink because Fonda Pepe is situated so practically along the main road. And if the hundreds of guests that come here on pleasant summer evenings don't leave a space for you, you can always sit outside on the wall in front of the bar with the others.

Those who harbor dreams of building their own guitar can finally make them come true by participating in one of the holiday courses on offer at *Formentera Guitars* in Sant Ferran.

Many years ago Bob, a New Yorker, set up the *Biblioteca Internacional* here – a library of donated books. It holds over 25,000 volumes in ten languages.

Following Bob's death in 1996 the town of Sant Francesc took over the colorful stock.

The small, colorful stalactite cave of ***Cova d'en Xeroni**, 1 kilometer southeast of Sant Ferran's quarrystone church, is open for viewing. It is brightly illuminated and there is even a connecting bar.

A *tienda* (village store) between Sant Ferran and Platja Migjorn has been converted into a restaurant and will no doubt seduce you into rewarding yourself to a culinary stop: in the shade of some old fig trees the **La Tortuga** restaurant serves delicious roasted "Formenteran loin of pork" with cinnamon apples.

**Platja de Migjorn

The beautiful beach of ****Platja de Migjorn** ❻ covers almost the entire central south coast: over 6 kilometers of sand punctuated by rocky outcroppings and flanked by dunes, clean turquoise water and an agreeably small number of hotels and beach bars.

Formentera

Above: The Blue Bar – an institution since hippie times – on beautiful Platja de Migjorn.

Its western end near the resort of **Es Ca Mari** is known as **Platja de Formentera**. It is connected to the rock and sand beach of **Es Mal Pas** in the southwest and the sandy **Platja d'Els Arenals** with the resort clubs of **Maryland** and **Club La Mola** in the southeast.

The *Blue Bar** which dates all the way back to the hippie era is in a beautiful location and has a lovely terrace right beside the sea. The *Pirata Bus** beach bar is also a very popular venue. By the way, when a southerly wind blows some extremely dangerous currents can develop in parts of Platja de Migjorn.

The foundations of the **Castell Romà** (3rd century A.D.) recall the Roman era. It used to have 5 towers and measured 30 x 30 meters (10 kilometers, before reaching Es Caló).

Along the northern side of Formentera's "spine" the **Platja de Tramuntana**, sandy and interspersed by rocky outcroppings, is an excellent spot to indulge in some snorkeling. You can enjoy a meal or even spend the night in the small, friendly fishing town and resort of **Es Caló ❼**, a natural harbor with plenty of jetties and boat houses.

*La Mola Plateau

The main road winds its way from Es Caló to the plateau of La Mola, whose highest summit – **Sa Talaiassa** – lies at 192 meters. Along the way, after 14 kilometers, we can recommend a stop at the **Mirador** restaurant, if for no other reason than the superb view. You can also hike through the macchia up to the plateau on an old Roman road known as the **Camí Romà** which is only 1.5 kilometers long. Toward the top you'll notice that the landscape is subdivided by arid walls and the allotments are filled with fruit trees, vegetables and vines.

The hamlet of *El Pilar de la Mola ❽** is situated 155 meters above sea level and has a plain fortress church – the **Nuestra**

Senyora del Pilar, the comfortable **Can Toni** bar and the **Centro Artesania** where artists display and sell their works. Between May and September a hippie market – the ***Fira de la Mola** – takes place here on Wednesday and Saturday afternoons. Here you'll meet veteran flower children still attempting to make a living with their knitting, paintings and pottery creations.

Close to this small settlement is an old windmill called the ***Moli Vell de la Mola**, built in 1778.

The ***Far de la Mola ❾**, built in 1861, crowns the eastern edge of the island; the jagged coast falls away breathtakingly steeply at this point and is best avoided by those suffering from vertigo. In 1978 a monument was built here to honor the theoretical 150th birthday of Jules Verne, creator of that famous, fictitious world; a very noble gesture on the part of the islanders considering the Frenchman in his novel "*Off on a Comet*" (or "*Hector Servadac*" in French) let the "little island at the end of the world" collide with a comet and burn up.

*Cap de Barbaria and **Cala Saona

A road leads 8 kilometers from **Sant Francesc** to the southernmost point of the island: the wildly-romantic ***Cap de Barbaria ❿**. It is occupied by a lighthouse and the **Torre d'es Garroveret**, one of five still-preserved defense towers. It's gusty on this 100-meter-high cape; a few solitary goats graze on rosemary and thyme on this karstic land and even the aleppo pines seem weathered. There are no swimming possibilities; all you can do here (although it is rewarding) is gaze into the inky sea and listen to the cry of the gulls. If you really want to swim you can venture further north to the west coast, to the turquoise waters in the idyllic sand bay of ****Cala Saona ⓫**, where you'll find an eponymous hotel with a viewing terrace and a restaurant.

FORMENTERA

Oficina de Turisme, at La Savina harbor, tel. 971-322057, fax 322825; biking and hiking maps available free of charge, open Mon-Fri 10 am-2 pm, 5-10pm, Sat 10 am-2 pm.

The **express ferry** shuttles from Eivissa's harbor to Formentera almost hourly between 7:45 am and 8:30 pm; tickets cost about 6 U.S. dollars; the crossing takes approximately 30 minutes. A scheduled bus connects the harbor of Formentera with La Mola, and there are also taxis. Bicycles (at 4 dollars per day) and mopeds (from 14 dollars per day) can also be rented here.

Club Formentera Playa, Platja de Migjorn, tel. 971-320000; one of the best hotels on the island, 333 rooms, directly on the beach. **Club La Mola**, Platja Arenals, tel./fax 971-327000; 326 rooms, 66 of them in bungalows; tennis, water sports. **Club Maryland**, Platja de Migjorn, tel. 971-327111, fax 327145, 325 bungalows, pine tree-covered complex, 4 pools, disco, children's playground, tennis, entertainment. **Residencia Illes Pitiüses**, Avda. Joan Castelló Guasch 48-52, Sant Ferran, tel. 971-328189, fax 328017; small, friendly hotel, open all year, heating and air-conditioning. **Can Rafal**, Carrer Isidor Macabich, Sant Francesc, tel. 971-322205; first building on the square. **Cala Saona**, Platja Cala Saona, tel. 971-322030, fax 323509; on the peaceful, sandy bay.

Sa Volta, Carrer Espalmador s/n, Es Pujols, tel. 971-328228; *hostal* which is open all year, with heating and cafeteria. **Hostal Maysi**, Platja d'Es Arenals, tel. 971-328547, young clientele.

Sa Gavina, Platja de Es Pujols, tel. 971-328352; the "Seagull" is one of the best restaurants on Formentera specializing in Balearic cuisine and fresh seafood. **Es Molí de Sal**, Platja de Ses Illetes, cellphone 908-136773; popular, high-class fish restaurant in an old salt mill. **Las Ranas**, Sant Ferran, on the road to Cala en Baster, tel. 971-328195; French-style cuisine, beautiful terrace. Cafetería del Centro, Plaça de la Constitucion, Sant Francesc, tel. 971-320063; coffee and snacks opposite the church at the central square. **Fonda Pepe**, Carrer Mayor 40, Sant Ferran; an original, started as just a village bar but is now also a restaurant and hotel. **Blue Bar**, tel. 971-187011, on Platja de Migjorn, after 8 kilometers a signpost along the main road will direct you; Bob Dylan played his guitar on this terrace! Open noon til 4(!) am. **La Tortuga**, Carretera La Mola, 6 km, one of the best restaurants on the island; specialty of the house: delicious "Formenteran loin of pork."

Formentera

ACTIVE HOLIDAYS

Cycling: Those wishing to see the real face of the Pitiusas should pedal. On **Formentera** the bicycle is undoubtedly the best mode of transport for tourists. Even Bob Dylan explored the island from the comfort of a saddle. Those coming by ferry from Ibiza will see several bike rentals upon arrival who offer bone-shakers at very favorable rates. We recommend you always check the technical condition of the bike beforehand. As Formentera is almost completely flat self-propulsion on two air-padded wheels proves to be both comfortable and fun. This island is better explored by bicycle in the fresh air than from the inside of a car and a map of cycle routes is available in the tourist information office at the harbor of La Savina.

Preceding pages: Preparing paella for the village festival is a man's job. Above: Formentera is best explored by bike. Right: There is an extensive range of water sports available at Platja d'En Bossa (Ibiza).

Ibiza, on the other hand, is very hilly and anyone cycling there will need to be fit and should take extra care to avoid the often very narrow, busy roads. Equipped with a sturdy mountain bike and a *Rutas en Mountain Bike* brochure, which can be picked up in any tourist office, you'll find yourself undergoing a sudden transformation in pine forests and mutating into enthusiastic boy scouts and girl guides; along the routes you'll come across rare species of plants and find some nice quiet spots, for example secluded bays. Sometimes the coast falls hair-raisingly steeply to the sea below, which is usually easily reached: all you have to do is hop off your bike, throw your clothes aside and dive into the crystal-clear waters.

To get used to the exercise take the pleasant cycle route south of Eivissa town. It leads through the **Ses Salines** area where the oldest industry on the island is still carried out: salt extraction. It is also under nature conservation so cars are not permitted. A new bicycle trail connects **Sant Jordi** with the small village of **La Canal**. You'll find yourself cycling through ancient salt flats, spotting a whole variety of birds feeding in dammed-up bodies of water and admiring the fascinating salt deposits which have formed along the edge. If you cycle here in the evenings you'll get to experience very impressive sunsets.

Hiking: Ibiza, with its forested hills, dramatically-steep coasts and tranquil bays, has distinguished itself in the last few years as an exciting destination for hikers, mostly outside the peak season. Trails are marked by colored guideposts upon which a falcon is depicted. The *Ruta de Falcón* markings lead all over the island and local tourist authorities have published a hiking brochure which is available in tourist offices. Backpacking holidays, as opposed to only sun and sea holidays, present visitors with an excellent opportunity to not only explore the flora and fauna of the island but also to

get to know the natives; visitors restricting themselves to the tourist ghettos will never, or very rarely, get to meet a local. In stark contrast to the resorts, tourists traveling the island *per pedes* simply won't be able to avoid encounters with the authentic face of Ibiza and will see locals at work and play, meet families out on day trips and entire village communities flocking to church on Sundays. With a bit of luck and a little Spanish you'll be able to strike up a conversation with them. And only those traveling on their own steam will truly understand how rural and unspoilt this island really is, because some parts remain untouched by mass tourism even if they're located very close to the major tourist centers.

Some of the old roads used by hikers were built by shepherds and goatherds in prehistoric times and they were widely used by the Carthaginians and subsequently by the Romans and Arabs. Those who walk will have the history of this small nation revealed to them with every self-propelled step.

One of the most beautiful hiking routes is the ascent to the highest mountain summit – **Sa Talaia** – at 475 meters, which can be reached via a small trail from **Sant Josep**. From the summit you can enjoy breathtaking panoramic views over the southern part of the island and if you still have energy to spare you can continue on to the beautiful sand bay of **Cala d'Hort**.

Another recommended walk is in the north – **Sant Miquel** and surroundings. The dazzling white courtyard in the impressive fortress church is still the heart of the town to this day, particularly so on Sundays. The frescoes inside it are only a recent discovery. After seeing the church continue on to **Port de Sant Miquel** from where you'll get a fine view of the churning seas below.

You can walk along the steep and varied north coast from **Portinatx** to **Cala Xarraca** in only three hours, then continuing on to the cape of **Punta Xarraca**.

Sant Llorenç de Balàfia is an especially well-preserved little village. Three fortress towers overlook the crowded cluster of white houses, as villages had to be adequately fortified in those days to combat the spreading plague of piracy. There are more of these striking watchtowers in the village's surrounding countryside.

Hiking around **Sant Mateu** is highly recommended in January and February. From the gentle ridges you'll be rewarded with breathtaking views of valleys overflowing with almond trees which are in full blossom at this time of year.

Hiking from bay to bay is also a wonderful way to get around. It takes two hours to walk to **Es Canar** from the yacht harbor in **Santa Eulària**. The trail along the southwestern coast is just as long and runs from **Cala Bassa** to **Cala Codolar**. Along the way there are several beautiful bays to investigate and you'll have a hard time deciding which one is your favorite.

Golf: Ibiza is by no means a paradise for golfers. The only course is difficult as its green is rather hilly and has several water obstacles. A second course is being planned near Cala d'Hort, but the project is being vehemently opposed by conservationists. So for now the 27-hole course at **Roca Llisa** will have to do; it is a challenge for experienced golfers and downright difficult for beginners. But its stunning location with breathtaking views compensates its difficulty.

Sailing: Ibiza is ideal territory for all kinds of water sports and the mild climate here means that sailing and windsurfing can be enjoyed throughout the year. Those who know their way around the moods of the sea and wind can swim here all year round. One general rule can always be applied to this island: those seeking calm waters should head for the leeward side of the island, i.e. out of the direction of the wind (usually the southeast). Those wishing to sail or windsurf should head for the windward side where

Right: Departing for a diving excursion (Port de Sant Miquel).

they can make the most of the full force of the wind (usually the northwestern side of the island). Windsurfing and sailing instruction with board and boat rental is usually available on all the major beaches. Larger boats can be chartered at Eivissa's yacht harbor (for example at *Coral Yachting*, tel. 971-313926).

Diving: Divers will be able to enjoy close encounters in underwaterscapes lush with swaying marine flora, schools of colorful fish, barracuda, perch, moonfish, crabs, corals and other marine life in clean, crystal-clear waters with an impressive visibility of up to 40 meters. November, January and March are considered the best months for diving because the waters of the western Mediterrean are especially clear during this time. The most popular diving territories are below the steep cliff faces of the **Es Vedrà** and **Sa Conillera** islets in the west, **Tagomago** in the east and **Ses Margalidas** and **Murada** in the north. The whole northwestern coast of Ibiza presents a magical underwater world which will send even seasoned divers into raptures. For even more thrills you can head for the "enchanted" shipwrecks which can be reached from many of the diving bases.

Swimming: The island's 56 beaches measuring 18 kilometers in total are Ibiza's premier asset. It is the ultimate destination for keen swimmers and sun-worshippers because the island is small and its beaches and bays are easily accessible from every hotel and resort. Coastal regions are usually under nature conservation and are always kept clean. Only a few areas have been badly developed, evidenced by the unsightly offspring of the 1970s concrete boom. However, since the conservative *Partido Popular* was replaced by a red-green coalition in 1999 the links bonding politics and the building industry have been weakened; the importance of environmental protection has finally been recognized here and an

environmental tax has even been introduced. All the undeveloped coastal regions have a 500-meter-wide green belt under specific environmental protection; excavators and bulldozers must remain outside these protected zones.

Ibiza also possesses image-oriented beach areas such as **Platja d'en Bossa** and **Platja de Ses Salines** southwest of Eivissa, where the young and beautiful sport daring beachwear and revel in their mutual flirt rituals. Topless sunbathing is the norm, the mood is relaxed, both machos and beach babes are happy to exhibit themselves in exchange for some external admiration; a musical, liberal, sensual beach world. No wonder then that the beaches (including Sant Antoni) are completely overcrowded.

The gay scene meets up at the southern end of **Platja d'Es Cavallet** near the Chiringay bar. Naturists will also find suitable territory there, as well as **Aigua Blanca** in the island's northeast and **Platja de ses Illetes** on Formentera's northern tip. The islands are renowned for their tolerance; those not behaving conspicuously or offensively can move around freely and sunbathe "as nature intended" on any of the more out-of-the-way beaches.

But even those preferring seclusion will get their money's worth here. Ibiza's north and east conceals tiny rock bays which make a close encounter with nature at its most pristine an experience to be reckoned with. Sometimes these spots of tranquility can only be reached by daringly courageous descents. The water is always clear to a considerable depth and the underwaterscapes are fascinating. Sharks do not pose a threat here.

Family beaches are also abundant. There are plenty of shallow bays where parents can doze in their deckchairs whilst keeping an eye on their offspring creatively engaging in the art of sandcastle building, and the water is nothing short of pure pleasure. A blue EU environmental flag flies on many Ibizan beaches and indicates especially clean water.

Active Holidays

NIGHTLIFE

Party animals, night owls and thrill-seeking contemporaries will experience Ibiza as an *Isla Magica* every night in high season. Hardly any other place possesses such an array of bars, pubs, discos and trendy hangouts in such a small space. Ibiza is just one huge open-air party in summer, while on Formentera the nights tend to be far more peaceful.

A few smart business people turned **Sant Antoni** into the party capital by establishing some very classy discos. By the 1980s this nocturnal virus had attacked the whole island and a range of high-class establishments opened their thundering gates to the public, including the gigantic **Ku** (today the **Privilege**) with room for 7,000 guests, the **Pacha** with room for 3,000 over three floors and **Es Paradis**, among others. And when DJs from London and elsewhere discov-

Above: "Pacha" in Eivissa's yacht harbor can accommodate 3,000 dancing guests.

ered these techno temples Ibiza became a very hot tip in the global trend scene.

All inhibitions are wiped away in the hot Ibizan nights. Presenting oneself as suitably hip or dressing up in completely strange costumes to resemble an off-the-wall human bird of paradise is also the norm. And most people are more than happy to pay up to 50 dollars to get into an open-air superparty in one of the club discotheques.

The first early evening stop is normally **Café Montesol** or **Mar y Sol** near the harbor of **Eivissa**, which undergoes a transformation at night when the disciples of fun are infused with nocturnal impetus. They've squeezed themselves into tight leather or have playfully applied body paint; they're displaying lots of flesh whilst exhibiting some extremely daring creations; especially the drag queens. And the locals smile knowingly and calmly take stock of the *poco locos* – the crazies who have invaded their town.

The **KM5** is a good place for warming up, followed by the **Manumission Mo-**

tel. At "disco time" after midnight the party people meet up again at a variety of venues where they are absorbed into the raving crowds of dancers and exhibitionists. Megadiscos like **Privilege**, **Pacha** and **Amnesia** have huge dance floors, a Caipirinha costs over four dollars, flirting is a multilingual experience, narcotics aid the susceptible through temporary low points and add a little extra energy to an otherwise unsatisfactory physical encounter. The **El Divino** is more classy.

Those still unquenchable by morning who still haven't had enough of the dancing, flirting, groping and foam that gets sprayed around the discos, can go to **Konga** or **Space** directly beneath the airport's approach corridor. They don't open until the other discos have closed, i.e. after sunrise. Ambulances belonging to the Ibizan Red Cross are permanently stationed outside the front doors, the bouncers here are tougher than the Guardia Civil and most of the society set just doze their way in, completely over-exhausted but proudly aware that they've outdone themselves once again. Their only hope now is a coffee in **Croissant Show**.

Ibiza's nightlife is spectacular, but quieter nights are possible too. Some are attracted to the jingling slot machines in the **Casino de Ibiza** at dusk. Others drive to Sant Rafel to the **Hipódromo Ibiza**, a racing course with entertainment rooms where one can take dinner whilst watching the colorful jockeys tearing forth on their horses – until 2:30 am. Naturally one could also make a few bets.

In Eivissa you can even experience a musically cultural evening, e.g. in **Teatro Pereira** – a former movie theater now transformed into a design artwork in natural stone and brass. The Dutch impresario Eric-Jan Harmsen made the **La Cantina** *the* fashionable place to go and he invites exceptionally-gifted musicians, usually soloists, to perform here.

Sant Antoni's nightlife conforms to its own laws. Its snack bars and pubs with their colorful signs at the harbor and in the West End are jampacked until midnight, after which the party people move on to the **Eden** or the classy **Paradis**, one of Ibiza's most beautiful dance temples.

On the other hand, **Santa Eulària** or the third "city" is still relatively relaxed at night by comparison. Megadiscos: nothing doing. Young people coo on the promenade, gazes are exchanged in the cafés and bars and the dignified elderly enjoy a dance on the open-air parquet.

Those unwilling to dance or sway to the music can entertain themselves by observing the Rolex set play their social spiel in **Café Sidney** in **La Marina**, the yacht harbor of **Eivissa**. An armada of valuable automobiles is parked in front of it, thousands of carats flash in the dark like trophies and the champagne flows in rivers beneath spotlights sparkling almost as brightly as the people beneath them.

Ibiza's annual party assault has not only given it Europe's largest discotheques – gigantic dance factories with several-thousand-watt sound systems, pools, laser shows, foam guns, tattoo parlors and night boutiques – but also a DJ cult. Around 500 DJs gather on the island every season, spin their chrome discs and hope the industry's trend scouts will discover them so they can get a contract and revel in stardom. That's how DJ José Padilla found fame and fortune. Many European department stores now play his mellow tunes, which were heard first in the **Café del Mar** in Sant Antoni between 1991 and 1996. And the jet set still flocks there at night, when the sun sinks behind the sea and Sant Antoni's more unsightly buildings are bathed in a soft red glow. During moments like these the disciples of dance, just like the hippies in their day, enthuse about how this beautiful world must still be worth saving.

Information on nightlife is available on the web: www.ibizanight.com. Between midnight and 6 am a disco bus shuttles to and from the out-of-town megadiscos.

Nightlife

HIPPIE MARKETS

The hippie movement – once a world-wide zeitgeist phenomenon which had a powerful psycho-social effect on the development of modern western culture ("make love, not war") – dissolved in the arcana of the New Age movement. But remnants of flower power euphoria are still preserved on Ibiza today. The first hippie market took place in 1972 on the grounds of the Punta Arabi holiday club in Es Canyar. The self-pronounced outcasts banged their drums and tambourines here, smoked their pot, plucked their guitars, all the while humming "The answer, my friend...", threw their full manes of hair around them whilst tidying their jumble of home-made leather bands, aluminum, copper and crochet work which they used to adorn their necks and

Above: A wide range of essential oils are available in the hippie market at Las Dalias. Right: Drum roll for the market shoppers in Punta Arabi near Santa Eulària.

arms and offered all their handicrafts at very humane prices.

It is still like that today, though it must be said that the handicrafts have become overshadowed by plastic junk and kitschy knick-knacks. Modern-day hippie markets are by no means represented by only flower children. Whole convoys of Europe-wide traders have gained a strong foothold here and fashion designers also find this a suitable selling environment in which to offer their creations.

Punta Arabi has become a huge bazaar with about 400 stands in all, and between Easter and Thanksgiving the Ibizan bus operators cart throngs of tourists here to buy leather goods, jewelry in all shapes and forms including the unimaginable, wood, glass and ceramic crafts as well as the usual unavoidable array of products "made in Taiwan." Gypsies also trade here, specializing in leather belts, bags, vests and African jewelry made of wood. Wheeler-dealers make a killing selling airy Indian dresses, floppy hats, musical instruments or fashionable odds and ends. Rarities and truly valuable objects can hardly be found here at all, but it is still charmingly atmospheric to experience the last remaining specimens of this colorful but almost extinct species still debating about how the world could be a better place with the help of flower power, while they enjoy a mellow smoke. But their faces telltale the toll of their lifestyle: they are marked by deep grooves and their teeth have been discolored by the tobacco in their hash rolls. "Hippie-watching" has become a tourist pastime and the victims in question either play along or not at all, bravely holding their own as the veterans of a subculture that once rocked the globe.

Hippie markets take place in several towns on a weekly basis in peak season. They are the trademark of Ibiza and remind us that the bliss of hippiedom has managed to survive in some small biotopes, where one can get a tattoo, have

colorful cotton ribbons plaited into one's hair, make music, play marbles with the kids or have one's freshly-mixed tarot cards read by a fortune-teller. Tortillas and sangria can be obtained cheaply here, meaningful aphorisms free of charge, and fun is had by all. For markets check out **Sant Miquel** on Thursdays, **Platja d'en Bossa** on Fridays and **Las Dalias** near Sant Carles on Saturdays, although real craftsmanship is more likely to be found at Sant Miquel and Las Dalias. On Wednesdays and Sundays there is an authentic hippie market in **El Pilar** on Formentera, where most of the goods really are home-made. Mobile stalls with colorful bits and pieces are also set up in the harbor zones of most Ibizan towns, in pedestrian zones and in some town lanes.

Thousands of flower children once lived on these islands. Many of them adapted to the Pitiusas lifestyle and stayed for good. They have since become successful self-made men or businesswomen; they've opened bars and boutiques or invested their creative talents in fashion design or hotel management. Anthony Pike, a seasoned globetrotter from Australia, turned a former olive press near Sant Antoni into an exclusive finca hotel. The insatiably libidinous Mick Jagger and Julio Iglesias broke their marital vows here and aimlessly meandering aristocrats have made history here with their wild orgies, while other VIPs are currently trying to cope with their umpteenth marriage partner. The legend that those entering their own beautifully-secluded flophouse will be met with the ultimate service, at a price of course, is well and truly alive; the rest is up to one's imagination. Those rooms once frequented by the Spanish crooner and British rock star are usually booked out.

An aura of hippiedom was always present on the Pitiusas, long before the invasion of the flower children actually took place. *Tranquil* is a word the islanders use to refer to the soothing effect of listening to the sounds of the sea, a gentle, natural tune that inspires something inside us to sway to its rhythm.

IBIZAN CUISINE

The cuisine of the Pitiusas is essentially Mediterranean; wheat, olive oil and wine comprise its basis. Fish and meat, eggs, milk, rice, beans, vegetables, fruit and dried fruit are used most often. These ingredients are combined in the most varying and imaginative ways, resulting in vitamin-packed, delicious dishes. Many former colonizers have left their mark in Ibizan and Formenteran cooking – Phoenicians and Greeks, Romans, Arabs and Spaniards. But the characteristic aromatic wild herbs present in most dishes are indigenous to the Pitiusas and represent the flavor of the island.

When we consider that Ibiza is swamped by 1.8 million tourists annually it's only natural that international cuisine,

Above: Butifarra (blood sausage) and Sobrasada (pork sausage) – vital ingredients for sofrit pagès. Right: Fresh fish and seafood served right on Platja de Ses Illetes on Formentera.

including everything from Chinese stir-fries to French haute cuisine, should also be available here. And because of this culinary diversity it's not half as easy as one might think to identify and explore original local cooking, as many gastronomers seem to think that foreign guests are fundamentally geared toward pizza, fish'n'chips, wiener schnitzel and black forest gateau. In addition, there is a little embarrassment associated with Ibizan cooking because it is more wholesome and solid than the more refined nouvelle cuisine. Despite this, it is a fact that well-prepared Pitiusan dishes can be a wonderful culinary experience.

The substantial use of natural island produce can result in the creation of, for example, *sofrit pagès*: a powerful, rustic stew incorporating chicken, lamb, pork and coarse sausages – *butifarra* (blood sausage) and *sobrasada* (pork sausage) – with potatoes, garlic, cloves, parsley, pepper, saffron and cinnamon, which simmers on the stove until almost all the liquid has turned into a kind of mush. *Sofrit*

pagès is prepared in a large pot, but should not be stirred; the pot must instead be shaken. Over the course of time this colorful ragout has been refined and incorporated into the menus of many restaurants, but it is nevertheless still jampacked with tasty calories. Whoever has the pleasure of tasting this delicious dish will be more than satisfied. And even if the *sofrit pagès* turns out to be a little heavier on the stomach than previously anticipated it still ranks as No.1 on the list of the most popular island dishes.

But the challenge lies not in eating but in finding a restaurant that serves original island cuisine. What you'll find most often are foreign-owned tourist traps open only for the main season which have attractive menus but serve meals that induce an immediate feeling of regret. "Tourist menus" should be avoided at all costs – wherever you are in the world – but especially in Mediterranean regions. The food in these places is usually carelessly prepared, resulting in a concoction that looks and tastes flat and boring. So,

although the menus featuring greasy fries and sardines have been overhauled, you should still do a little investigating if you want to eat out well.

One general rule always applies: fresh fish and seafood are of the highest quality in small seaside restaurants run by natives. You get to see the freshly-caught fish beforehand and explain how you would like it prepared. Rural specialties, above all lamb dishes, are a highly-recommendable delicacy in restaurants in the island's interior. They are usually family-run establishments where mothers and grandmothers still dominate the stove. It is as good as guaranteed that the food in these places will taste wonderful.

Meat dishes are often refined by adding delicious herbs, which make them even tastier and harder to resist. On public holidays the natives go to great lengths to prepare *lechona asada*: suckling pig encrusted with herbs. *Conill amb ceba* is a dish incorporating rabbit and lots of onions. Pan-fried *frita pagesa* is prepared with pork and liver in a stock of red pep-

81

pers, garnished with mushrooms and garlic and then complemented with an accompaniment of fried potatoes.

Seafood is naturally plentiful on these islands. *Guisat de peix* is a potent fish stew prepared with almonds, potatoes and saffron – just the way the locals like it. Tuna with eggs and pine kernels, pickled in dry white wine and lemon juice, is served in the restaurants under the name *tonyina al' eivissenca*. Another seafood dish typical for these islands is *borrida de rajada*: ragout of ray served in an almond sauce. Swordfish has been relished on Ibiza as early as Punic times and *garum* – a fish paste made of anchovies (made famous by the Carthaginians and later finding fame in the entire Mediterranean region) – used to accompany it.

Paella, which can be found all around the Mediterranean in one form or another,

Above: A choice of delicious cakes in Sant Josep de Sa Talaia. Right: Hierbas ibicencas, the island's very own herb liqueur, is said to be a cure-all.

is known as *arròs sec* on the Pitiusas. The local variation includes rice and mussels, prawns, chicken and vegetables, sometimes even rabbit. Some of the delicious *tapas*, for example *frita de polp* (squid stew) or *freixura*, made with innards, also convey the archetypal taste of the Pitiusas. *Caragols sofregits* are baked snails which are eaten with the aid of a tooth pick as an in-between snack. *Coca*, a type of quiche filled with chard, peppers and fish, is available in most of the bakeries on Ibiza. *"Bon profit!"* ("bon appetit").

After a satisfying meal the locals like to order a *hierbas ibicencas*, a herb liqueur that aids digestion. This thick, amber-colored liquid, which sometimes shimmers a shade of green, has a host of herbs swimming in the bottle with it. It has a bittersweet taste and a soothing but simultaneously invigorating effect. The islanders claim that *hierbas* relieves stomach and intestinal upsets, helps one back on one's feet after a bout of gluttony and even acts as an antidote against

depression and lovesickness. It is also said to be an effective aphrodisiac.

Herbs and their products will follow you all over these islands. Old village herb-sellers are said to have performed feats resembling miracles with this natural produce. And any bartender worth his salt will have his own "secret" recipe for herb liqueur and he will happily swear by its properties. Some claim, with their two bottles a year, to have produced an absolutely unique version. But the production process really is time-consuming: the aniseed base is topped up with rosemary, juniper berries and a type of mountain mint, the rinds of locally-grown lemons and oranges and finally thyme and essential oils which play an important role. There are multitudes of recipes in circulation, but somehow the results all taste similar. This drink is an oral infusion of nature at its purest and as it is enriched with select wines the liqueur's alcohol content can be as high as 30 per cent. *Salud!* Sweeter variations of the drink are also available: *frigola* (with thyme) and *palo* (with ver-

mouth), all classic Ibizan creations. One special feature of these particular products is that they are said to not only taste delicious but also have medicinal properties which will alleviate both real and imaginary ailments.

Those with a taste for good red wines matured in oak casks will be spoilt for choice – the range includes fine Spanish wines, particularly those from Catalonia (*Penedés*) and the *Rioja* region. One especially fine product involving the noble grape is *cava*, that ever-popular Catalan sparkling wine which is produced according to the *méthode champenoise*. Wines which are locally produced, for example the dry *vi pagès* or the slightly sweeter *sa cova*, are relatively rare and are usually only available at local or family festivals. Wine is traditionally enjoyed straight from the *porrón*, a special long-necked bottle. There is no purity law here governing beer production, like there is in Germany for example, but the Spanish *San Miguel* and *Estrella* brands are nevertheless very good.

FLORA AND FAUNA

"This landscape," wrote Walter Benjamin to a friend "is the most pristine I have ever laid eyes on." That was back in 1932 when the famous German author and philosopher spent a few months on Ibiza. That was long before the tourist invasion, the hotel building boom and all its ecological consequences. But the dense prairies of seagrass (*posidonia oceanica*) off Ibiza's coast, an ecosystem providing food and shelter to a wide range of marine life, have remained pristine and were declared a UNESCO world heritage nature site in 1999.

The best time for nature lovers to visit Ibiza is spring, especially the months of March and April. Wild flowers in particular abound on Ibiza. Belonging in

Above: Pyramid orchids are only one of over 20 orchid species on Ibiza. Right: These days the podenco ibicenco (Ibizan greyhound) is being bred and sold again – at a very high price.

this category is the late-flowering narcissus (*narzissus serotinus*) with up to four flowers on each stem, which gives off a light, tangy scent. The Balearic horseshoe clover (*hippocrepis balearicum*) is quite common, especially since fewer goats are being kept on the island. One noteworthy botanical treasure is the fragile red-leafed snapdragon (*chaenorhinum rubrifolium formentera*) which peers out between the clefts of the rocky coast. Botanists consider the Ibizan thistle, classed as a weed in other European countries, to be a particular sensation because of its distinctive color: this island version is completely white (*cardus burgeanus ssp. ibicensis*). The gorse (*genista dorycnifolia*) and thyme (*thymus richardii*) varieties here are also endemic, which means that these species only exist here. There are also rare types of clove and Balearic St. John's wort, as well as Balearic cyclamen. Also endemic, the small origanum-shaped sunflower (*Helianthemum origanifolium*) hoists its way delicately through the sandy soil.

Plant fans will be enraptured by the rich orchid varieties on the Pitiusas. While islands with volcanic soil, e.g. the Canaries, are distinctly devoid of orchids, the fascinating plants feel right at home here on the limestone-rich soils of the Pitiusas. Furthermore, it has been proven that wild orchids cannot be replanted in foreign, domestic gardens, which is why they are better left alone so that they can be admired in their natural environment!

Ibiza's range of flora grew with the increasing number of new human arrivals. The Phoenicians imported the *sabina* (juniper cypress or juniperus phoenicia), pomegranate, olive and carob tree, the Arabs were accompanied by dwarf palms, citrus and almond trees and the Catalans brought the agave, fig cactus and potato with them. Forests once covered this island from coast to coast, long before it saw a human being. In early prehistoric times the aleppo pine, holm oak

and umbrella pine visually characterized the Pitiusas. Nowadays the *garigue* – a low-growing bush in abundant numbers, dominates the landscape; most of the original dense forests have been cut down. In summer the garigue dries out and the herbs and flowers wither, but these dried-out plants act like a protective layer and benefit tubers such as onions and the narcissus, lily and gladiola. Most species of orchid flourish within the *garigue*.

The Pitiusas are by no means rich in fauna, but at least there are no dangerous or poisonous animals. Centuries ago many domestic species were sent back into the wild to breed so that man would have something to hunt. Today common species on the islands include beech martens, hares, wild rabbits, falcons, ospreys, red-legged partridges, quails, gulls and flamingos, as well as many species of rats, mice and other rodents, but also the very rare genet (*genetta genetta*) which is Ibiza's most exotic mammal. The most varied family here is that of the birds.

Many of our feathered friends have found ideal conditions in these forests and bushes, salt pans and lakes. Fish are also abundant in the rich waters around the islands. The most famous reptile here is the Pitiusas lizard (*podarcis pitiusensis*), but it never attained the status of Ibiza's heraldic animal.

Quite unlike the *podenco ibicenco* or Ibizan greyhound, which is honored as a "living legacy of the past." This long-legged canine has a very slim body and pointed, erect ears. The ancestors of these noble creatures are reputed to have been introduced to the island by none other than Queen Cleopatra herself. It is said that she stopped here during a voyage to Rome; her greyhounds disembarked with her and some remained here and reproduced. Although this event was never proven the *podenco ibicenco*, faithful companion on many a rabbit hunt, is still there today. Once considered extinct they are now being bred again, and a male can fetch about 2,800 U.S. dollars.

METRIC CONVERSION

Metric Unit	US Equivalent
Meter (m)	39.37 in.
Kilometer (km)	0.6241 mi.
Square Meter (sq m)	10.76 sq. ft.
Hectare (ha)	2.471 acres
Square Kilometer (sq km)	0.386 sq. mi.
Kilogram (kg)	2.2 lbs.
Liter (l)	1.05 qt.

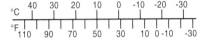

TRAVEL PREPARATION

Climate / Travel Season

The Pitiusas have a stable climate. Average annual temperatures are between 13.8 °C and 21.1 °C. A state of national panic breaks out if the mercury falls below 12 °C, but this only occurs every few years. Despite the islands' proximity to Africa temperatures rarely exceed 30 °C. Coastal regions are cooler in winter and more refreshing in summer than the interior. Statistically speaking the islands are blessed with an average 300 days of sunshine. Gray, rainy days are exceptional and a genuine novelty for the islanders. Meteorologists have recorded 59% sunshine hours, slightly more than Mallorca.

The islands are ideal for those dreaming of warmer climes in winter. In the "cold" season there are, on average, 5 hours of sunshine daily and southerly winds blow in a "little summer." It rains occasionally, but can also remain dry for several weeks. Water temperatures sink as low as 13 °C in winter. Spring is one of the most beautiful seasons, when the enchanting flora takes over. Summers are dry and taking a dip might be very refreshing if the water temperatures nudge the 24 °C mark. Summer evenings are mild. The first southwesterly winds arrive at the end of October, but you can still swim in the more sheltered bays where air temperatures remain at a pleasant 23 °C and water temperatures at 21 °C. October is said to have the highest precipitation levels, but this is not the rule. Autumn, when the islands blossom once more, is also a very good time to travel.

Clothing / Equipment

A light sweater always comes in handy in summer and sunglasses are recommended, as is sunscreen and a hat or cap, because the UV rays are very intense here. In winter you'll need practical clothing, i.e. water and wind-resistant. Locals dress smartly when they eat out, but generally one can dress casually and won't need much more than jeans, a shirt and light shoes. "*Vístete como quieras!*" means – "wear what you feel good in!" But what the locals don't like is tourists tripping through the streets of Eivissa in not much more than a tanga or men with bare torsos exhibiting tattoos and beer bellies. This form of exhibitionist won't be allowed to travel on buses in such an unsavory state and taxi drivers aren't actually permitted to ferry them from A to B either. This should be respected, for aesthetic and hygienic reasons.

Currency

Until 31st December 2001 the currency of Spain is the *peseta* (EPS). Notes circulate in denominations of 10,000, 5,000, 2,000 and 1,000 and coins in 500, 200, 100, 50, 25, 10, 5 and 1 peseta.

Rates of Exchange (at time of printing): 1 Euro = 166 EPS; 1 US Dollar = 186 EPS; 1 GB Pound = 267 EPS; 1 Australian Dollar = 96 EPS; 1 Canadian Dollar = 121 EPS; 1 Irish Punt = 211 EPS.

Cash-dispensers (*telebancos*) are everywhere and cash can be withdrawn with eurocheque and visa/credit cards, so the dispensers make a trip into the bank superfluous. Withdrawing cash is the cheapest way of obtaining local currency.

If the ATM is out of order you can withdraw up to 25,000 EPS by cashing a eurocheque (for a high fee) at the counter. Identification will be necessary.

All major credit cards are accepted by hotels, smart restaurants and fashionable places, but less so in the island's interior and in smaller shops.

Bank opening hours: Mon-Fri 9 am-2 pm, some banks also open Saturdays from 9 am-12:30 pm. The *bureaux de change* in the tourist centers are open longer.

Customs and Import Regulations

Most goods for personal use are not restricted within the EU. The following are restricted and only the given amounts may be brought into Spain from other EU countries: 800 cigarettes, 400 cigarillos or 200 cigars, 1 kg of tobacco, 10 l of spirits, 20 l of other alcoholic drinks (max. 22% alcohol content), 90 l of wine (max. 60 l of sparkling wine), 110 l of beer.

People entering Spain from non-EU countries may bring up to 10 kg of food and non-alcoholic drinks, 200 cigarettes or 250 grams of tobacco, and 1 l of spirits or 2 l of wine.

The same limits apply to goods bought from duty-free shops (airports, ferries) in a non-EU country before arrival in Spain, as well as from duty-free shops in Spain before arrival in a non-EU country. Duty-free shopping on journeys between EU countries has been abolished since 1999.

There are no restrictions on checks and travelers checks in foreign currencies or pesetas or other currencies in bank notes.

Entry Requirements / Visas

All you need to enter the country is a valid passport. Members of the EU need only their national ID card, which will be essential when checking into your hotel or renting a car.

Getting There By Plane

Inexpensive flights to Ibiza (via Barcelona or Mallorca) are available from most European airports with Iberia Airlines or national or seasonal charter airlines. Contact your local travel agent for details. Package deals usually work out cheaper.

An airport bus shuttles between the airport and Eivissa town at least once every hour between 7:30 am and 10:30 pm, a taxi into town costs around 2,500 EPS.

Getting There By Train

There are daily train connections to the Spanish mainland coast from most European cities; from there you can make the crossing over to Ibiza. For example, Munich to Barcelona via Zürich and Geneva takes about 19 hours and costs approx. 83 U.S. dollars or 58 GBP in second class. Prices in a sleeping car are about double.

Getting There By Car

Motorway tolls in France and the Spanish coast are high and considering ferry costs and the availability of small, cheap rental cars – which are ideal for the narrow, winding roads – it's not really worth bringing your own vehicle.

Getting There By Boat

Car ferries from Barcelona to Eivissa via Palma de Mallorca take 9½ hours. For information contact: Companía Trasmediterránea, Avda. Bart. Vicente Ramón 21, Eivissa, tel. 0034-971-315150 and 301650, www.trasmediterranea.es. Ferries from Deniá, south of Valencia at the Nao cape, are quicker. The modern hydrofoils make a beeline for Eivissa (or Sant Antoni) and take only four hours. Contact: Flebasa Edif. Faro I, Sant Antoni, tel. 0034-971-342871. Ferries operate regularly between Eivissa and Palma de Mallorca; contact: Trasmapi-Baleària, tel. 902-160180.

Information at: www.balearia.com

TRAVELING ON THE PITIUSAS

There is no railway; **buses** satisfy local transport needs. The network in Eivissa and Sant Antoni is satisfactory, but less so

Travel Information

in the island's interior. Getting a bus to one of the rural towns can be quite a challenge. Timetables are available in most hotels and tourist information offices.

There is no shortage of **taxis**. Eivissa, Sant Antoni and Santa Eulària des Ríu have plenty of public taxi stands, but in other places they must be called – tel. 971-307000 (your restaurant or hotel will be happy to do this). There are no meters, but lists of routes with fixed prices (arrange the price with your driver).

The **disco bus** is recommended. It runs from midnight until 6 am from June to September. Stops are along Avinguda Isidoro Macabich in Eivissa, Passeig de la Mar in Sant Antoni and in Santa Eulària on Avinguda Dr. Gotarredona.

There are plenty of **rental cars** from more than 30 rental companies; a few price comparisons are recommended. A small car costs about 3,500 EPS per day, not including tax and insurance. The best deals are usually all-inclusive. Comprehensive insurance is recommended as accidents can spark off complex legal proceedings for which you'll need to be covered. And it's equally important to check the state of your car beforehand. Maintenance quality can differ, so beware; sometimes the clutch will stick or the brakes may leave a lot to be desired. Hotel receptionists and tour guides know the best rental companies. If you want a car on arrival at the airport you should go to one of the better-known firms – their fleets are usually in good condition.

The police are on full alert at night due to increasing accidents over the past years. Drivers who have been drinking (the limit is 0.5%) are taken off the roads immediately and fines are extremely harsh. Other road offences must be paid on the spot in cash! **Speed limits**: on Ibiza it's 90 km/h on country roads, 50 km/h in towns; on Formentera it's 70 km/h on country roads, 50 km/h in towns. Using a cellphone whilst driving is prohibited.

Those not venturing far from their hotel can rent a **moped**. They are available on both islands and helmets are mandatory. **Bicycles** can also be rented everywhere, but they are less ideal for the Ibiza's narrow roads and should only be used on less busy roads. Formentera, on the other hand, is perfect for bikes.

Boats of differing price and class can be chartered in Eivissa, Santa Eulària des Ríu and Sant Antoni.

Ferries to Formentera run from Eivissa every 30 minutes between 7 am and 8 pm in high season, but also – although less often – from Sant Antoni and Santa Eulària. There are also water taxis.

PRACTICAL TIPS FROM A TO Z

Accommodation

All kinds of accommodation is available, but there is only one five-star hotel (*La Hacienda* near Sant Joan), although more of the luxury category are being planned. Prices have remained stable over the last few seasons. If you have any complaints you should contact the tourist office or your travel agent as quickly as possible – don't wait until you are at home. An increasing number of hotels are open all year round.

The symbols used at the end of each chapter can be interpreted as follows:

☉☉☉ = high-class to luxury: double rooms cost approx. 16,000 EPS per night (for two people).

☉☉ = middle-class: prices between 8,000 and 16,000 EPS.

☉ = simple: prices never exceed 8,000 EPS per night.

Hotels: from three stars upwards guests may expect air-conditioning and satellite TV. There are considerable differences in price even within the same category, but accommodation in tourist centers is generally cheaper than in the island's interior. Accommodation from tour operators has not been included here, but their package deals are usually good value.

Many of the hotels, hostals and pensions were renovated recently. On a plaque in every hotel lobby you'll see an "M" which stands for *"Hotel Modernitzat"* and the year the renovation took place. Official categories are: "H" for a normal hotel offering full board, "HR" for a *"Hotel Residencia"* offers half board but has an á-la-carte restaurant. "Hs" stands for pensions with breakfast, a *"Hostal Residencia"* is a pension with a restaurant. A "HA¨" is an apartment hotel offering self-catering apartments. "RA" represents *"Residencia Apartamentos"* – self-catering accommodation but with a restaurant. "CH¨" are *"Casa Huespedes"* – guesthouses offering only accommodation. "F" is a *"Fonda"* or country guesthouse which also offers food, but this is not included in the accommodation price.

Fincas are usually privately owned but rented out to friends and acquaintances. Some finca owners advertize in the island gazette and some European newspapers. The Ibiza House Renting Agency specializes in arranging finca accommodation: C/. Avicena 1, 07800 Eivissa, Ibiza, tel. 971-306213, fax: 305179.

Business Hours

Shops open at 9 or 10 am until 1 or 2 pm and again at 4 or 5 pm until 8 or 9 pm, but this can vary. In summer many boutiques remain open until midnight. Large supermarkets are open from 10 am til 10 pm, but close on Mondays. Country stores are usually open from 8 am, also on Sundays, but close at noon. Museums are closed on Mondays.

Camping

Five campsites are open from June to September: one in Sant Antoni, on in Cala Bassa and three near Es Canyar.

Children

Kids are the tourists of the future, therefore the tourist industry on these islands is increasingly adapting to their needs. Facilities for children have been dramatically improved in recent years and if you opt for a family trip to Ibiza and Formentera you'll be happy with the result. Hotels and club resorts are increasingly offering family-suited apartments and more travel agents than ever are putting together good value-for-money package deals. Parents and their offspring are no longer at the trying mercy of childcare and entertainment programs, rather the services on offer are becoming ever more varied and convenient. The islanders are friendly toward and take great care with children, so you needn't worry.

Crime

Pick-pocketing – a Spanish specialty – is rare on Ibiza and virtually non-existent on Formentera. But it is nevertheless sensible to take care with one's belongings. Robberies and murders are not a daily occurrence like they are in the touristic centers of Andalusia. What worries the authorities most are illegal immigrants, mostly from North Africa, who are said to play a major role in store raids.

Beware of tricksters, touts and pushers, of which there are plenty in Eivissa's harbor area. They will nag you until they get what they want. The best way to deal with them is to completely ignore them – boring them into submission is the only way.

The "tentacles" sent forth from the large clubs can be irritating; money is only made if the establishment is full, so they offer free entrance tickets. Some unsuspecting tourists honestly believe they've just been given 3,500 pesetas! Wrong. They want to get you through the disco doors and sufficiently tempted before charging you sky-high drinks prices.

But the mafia gangs controlling the drug trade present the biggest problem. Drugs are easy to come by despite spectacular measures taken in recent years. The pill-popping generation are easy prey here for designer drugs causing long-term brain damage.

Travel Information

A few simple guidelines will keep you out of trouble: keep valuables in your hotel safe, hand in your room key at reception. Don't bring large sums of cash to the beach or when out for the evening. Take everything out of your car before you lock it and try to park it in a car park with surveillance. By the way, car theft is rare on these islands (it's too expensive and troublesome to get the car off the island).

Disabled Tourists

The hotels and facilities on the Pitiusas are being systematically overhauled to suit disabled travelers. For more information contact your nearest Spanish Tourist Office or check out the internet site: www.tourspain.es

Electricity

The standard current in all hotels is 220 volts (50 cycles AC).

Emergencies

The telephone number for all emergencies is 112 and English is spoken. The number for ambulances is 061. Burglary and petty theft should be reported to the *Policía Nacional* at 091, road accidents must be reported to the *Policía Municipal* at 092. The fire brigade can be reached quickest by dialling 971-313030. The *Guardia Civil* has the number 062 on Ibiza, 971-322022 on Formentera.

Health

The sun's rays are intense, so sun cream with a high SPF (sun protection factor) should be compulsory. Even a day trip in an open car, on a moped or bicycle can result in bad sunburn. Eat light meals – the Mediterranean people have avoided heavy foods for millenia and know why. Your circulation will need to acclimatize, so it's a good idea to treat alcohol with caution. If you spot the locals enjoying a glass of red before noon be aware that they won't be knocking it back all night long! The tap water is good for drinking

(perhaps a little salty), but if you suffer from a sensitive stomach use your own supply of bottled water. AIDS didn't circumvent the Pitiusas, so it is not recommended to engage in sexual contact without taking the necessary precautions.

Holidays / Festivals / Events
Public Holidays:
January 1: New Year (*Ano nuevo*).
Januar 6: Epiphany (*Reyes magos*).
March 19: St. Joseph's Day.
March/April: Maundy Thursday (*Jueves Santo*) and Good Friday (*Viernes Santo*).
Mai 1: Day of Work (*Día del Trabajo*).
June: *Corpus Christi*.
June 24: Day of St. John and name day of King Juan Carlos of Spain.
June 25: Peter and Paul.
August 15: Assumption (*Asunsión*).
October 12: Spanish National Day (*Día de la Hispanidad*).
November 1: All Saints (*Todos los santos*).
December 8: Immaculate Conception (*Inmaculada Concepción*).
December 25/26: Christmas (*Navidad*).
December 31: Balearic Day (*Día de las Balears*) and New Year's Eve.
All shops and businesses are closed on these days.

Internet Cafés and Addresses

Postcards are passé for some: nowadays it's "cool" to send your holiday greetings electronically. You can check and send e-mail at: **Eivissa** on Av. Ignacío Wallis 39, tel. 971-318161, www.centrointernet eivissa.com (400 EPS for 30 minutes), in **Sant Antoni** in the service shop on Av. Dr. Fleming 1, tel. 971-348712, www.e-biza.net (250 EPS for 15 minutes).

Useful internet addresses:
www.tourspain.es
www.ibiza-spotlight.com
www.global-spirit.com/ibiza
www.ibiza-online.com
www.santaeulalia.net

www.spainalive.com
www.ibizanight.com
www.bluerose-ibiza.com
www.guiaformentera.com
www.mma.es (aerial views of beaches)

Language and Place Names

Since 1983 all the signposts on Ibiza and Formentera have been changed into *Eivissenc*, a dialect of Catalan and the original language of the islands. We've compiled a small list of the most prominent place names in Catalan and Castilian (high Spanish, second official language):

Ciutat Eivissa / Ciudad de Ibiza
Sant Agustí / San Agustín
Sant Antoni / Sant Antonio
Sant Carles / San Carlos
Sant Ferrán / San Fernando (Formentera)
Sant Frencesc / San Francisco (Formentera)
Sant Josep / San José
Sant Joan / San Juan
Sant Lorenc / San Lorenzo
Sant Mateu / San Mateo
Sant Rafel / San Ráfael
Sant Vicent / San Vicente
Santa Eulària des Ríu / Santa Eulalia del Rio

However, this "Catalanizing" doesn't appear to have been carried out thoroughly or uniformly, e.g. one single bay now has several different descriptions such as Es Canar, Es Caná or Es Canya. The reason: although "standard" Catalan is the official language of the region hardly anybody speaks it; instead they speak their own regional variation, e.g. Northern Catalan, Northwestern Catalan, Central Catalan, Valencian or *Balearic*, and on Ibiza one of 5 sub-dialects, namely *Eivissenc*. The largest tour operators usually use Spanish names for towns and Catalan names for beaches and bays.

Pronunciation of Balearic Catalan:

ca, que, qui, co, cu · *ka, ke, kee, ko, koo*
ça, ce, ci, ço, çu . . . *sa, se, see, so, soo*
qua, qüe, qüi, quo. . *kwa, kwe, kwi, kwo*
ga, gue, gui, go, gu . *ga, ge, gee, go, goo*
ja, jo, ju . . . . *sha, sho, shoo*
ge, gi. . . . . *shé, shee*
gua, güe, güi . . . . *gua, gué, gui*
ll. *ly*
x, tx. . . . . *sh, tsh*
tg, tj . . . . *tsh* (platja=*platsha*)
uig, aig, oig, eig . . *utsh, atsh, otsh, etsh*
. . . . (puig=*putsh*)
z. . . . . pronounced *s*
ei, eu . . . . *é-i, é-oo*

Lost and Found

There are no official "Lost Property" offices. If you've lost something you should go to the police station and ask there. And if you find anything, that's also the place to hand it in.

Medical Treatment

Most medical practitioners and their staff speak English. You'll find details of British or at least English-speaking practitioners and dentists in the local English information magazines or you can ask at your hotel reception. Private holiday health insurance, which should also cover any family traveling with you, is highly recommended.

Eivissa's state hospital is the **Hospital Can Misses**, tel. 971-397000. There is also a hospital in Formentera – the **Centro Medico** in Sant Francesc, tel. 971-322369 – and there is an emergency helicopter service to Ibiza.

Naturism / Nudism

Ibiza's official naturist beaches are the Platja des Cavallet near the salinas, Aigua Blanca in the northeast and Platja de ses Illetes located on the northern tip of Formentera. The islands are renowned for their tolerance. Topless sunbathing is accepted everywhere and those not behaving conspicuously or offensively may bathe and sunbathe nude at most of the more out-of-the-way beaches. But it isn't acceptable to go nude on family beaches or near built-up areas or beach restaurants.

Travel Information

91

Pets

Stray canines are usually shooed away on beaches but the islanders have nothing against visitors bringing their furry friends on holiday with them. It is compulsory to present a certificate from your vet, no more than two weeks old, stating that your pet is in good health and was vaccinated against rabies no longer than 30 days ago.

Pharmacies

Well-stocked pharmacies (*farmácias*) can be found in most towns and have signs outside with a green cross on a white background. All the usual medication is available, many without prescription. Opening times are the same as for shops. Details of emergency medical services are displayed on the door of every farmácia. If you require special medication you should bring enough with you.

Photography

Film is available in all the towns and villages, but it is expensive so bring enough with you from home. If you opt have your films developed on the islands you'll be pleased with the high-quality results. But take heed before "shooting" people: ask their permission first – just point meaningfully at your camera and wait for the nod. Please respect the wishes of old women in dark or traditional clothing if they don't want to be photographed.

Postal Services

Post offices are open from 9 am to 2 pm, Saturdays until noon. Stamps can also be bought in tobacco shops (*estanc*) and some newspaper and magazine stands. Postcards and standard letters to Europe cost 37 U.S. cents or 26 British pence. Letters to European countries take about a week. If you're staying longer you can get your post and newspapers sent "poste restante" or "general delivery" from home to your resort – "*en llista de*

correos." Eivissa's main post office (*correus*) can be found in C/. Madrid. Postman is delivered and collected only twice a week in the island's interior.

Press / Media

All the English-language daily and weekly newspapers and magazines are available on the day of publication. They will be more expensive than at home.

Telecommunications

The telecom company *Telefónica* is a private enterprise independent of the post office. Its central office in **Eivissa** is at the corner of C/. Canaris and C/. Aragón and is open every day from 8 am until 10 pm, including Saturdays. A 4-minute phone call to Europe from here or from one of the many phone boxes stationed around the beaches costs around 1,000 pesetas – cheaper than most cellphone calls. Calls are 25 per cent cheaper between 10 pm and 8 am, as well as from 2 pm on Saturdays until 8 am on Monday mornings.

The former area code for the Balearics is now integrated into all locals numbers and must always be dialled. If you want to call Ibiza or Formentera from abroad you must dial 0034 for Spain and then the 971 before the local number. If you want to make a local call you must also dial the 971. Cellphones don't begin with 971 but with 6. For international calls dial 001 for U.S.A. and Canada, 0044 for the United Kingdom, 00353 for the Republic of Ireland, 0061 for Australia and 0064 for New Zealand, followed by the area code without the 0 and then the local number.

Television

All the better hotels are equipped with satellite receivers, so the international channels are usually available.

Time Zone

The Pitiusas have Central European Time (CET). The clock also changes for summer and winter: on the last weekend in March the clocks are set back one hour (for summer) and in the last weekend in October they are set forward one hour.

Tipping

Services charges are included in restaurant bills. Nevertheless, a tip of around 10 per cent of the final charge is in order. Service personnel don't earn a lot so they might depend on your tips. If the bill is large the tip you give should not exceed 300 EPS. Porters should be given 100 EPS per luggage item and just round up the fare to tip your taxi driver.

USEFUL ADDRESSES

Diplomatic Representation in Spain

AUSTRALIA: Embassy of Australia, Plz. Del Descubridor Diego de Ordás 3, 28003 Madrid, tel. +34-91-4419300, fax: +34-91-4425362.

CANADA: Canadian Honorary Consulate, P. de Gracia 77, C.P. 08008 Barcelona, tel. +34-93-2150704.

IRELAND: General Consulate of Ireland, Gran Vía Carlos III 94, Torre "Oeste" Planta 10-C.P. 08028 Barcelona, tel. +34-93-3309652.

NEW ZEALAND: Honorary Consulate of New Zealand, Travesera de Gracia 64, 08006 Barcelona, tel. +34-93-2090399.

U.K.: British Vice Consulate, Isidoro Macabich 45, 1-07800 Ibiza, tel. +34-971-301818.

U.S.A.: General Consulate of the United States of America, P. Reina Elisende de Moncatde 23, C.P.-08034 Barcelona, tel. +34-93-2802227.

Spanish Embassies Abroad

AUSTRALIA: Spanish General Consulate, Level 24, St. Martin's Tower, 31 Market St., Sydney, N.S.W. 2000 Sydney, tel. +61-2-92612433, fax: +61-2-92831695.

CANADA: Spanish Embassy, 74 Stanley Avenue, Ottawa (Ontario), K1M 1P4,

Ottawa, tel. +1-613-7472252, fax: +1-613-7441224.

IRELAND: Embassy of Spain, 17A Merlyn Park, Ballsbridge, Dublin 4, tel. +353-1-2691640, +353-1-2691854.

U.K.: Spanish General Consulate, 20 Draycott Avenue, London SW3 2SB, tel. +44-20-75898989, fax: +44-20-

U.S.A.: Spanish General Consulate, 150 East 58th St., 30th Floor, New York, NY 10155, tel. +1-212-3554080, fax: +1-212-6443751.

Tourist Offices of Spain Worldwide
Internet: http://www.tourspain.es

CANADA: 2 Bloor Street West - 34th Floor, Toronto, Ontario M4W 3E2, tel. +1-416-9613131, fax: +1-416-9611992, www.tourspain.toronto.on.ca, e-mail: toronto@tourspain.es

U.K.: 22-23 Manchester Square, London W1U 3PX, tel. +44-20-74868077, fax: +44-20-74868034, www.tourspain.co.uk (or) www.uk.tourspain.es, e-mail: londres@tourspain.es

U.S.A.: 666, Fifth Avenue, New York, NY 10103, tel. +1-212-2658822, fax: +1-212-2658864, www.okspain.org, e-mail: nyork@tourspain.es

8383 Wilshire Blvd, Suite 960, Beverly Hills, CA 90211, tel. +1-323-6587188, fax: +1-323-6581061, www.okspain.org, e-mail: losangeles@tourspain.es

PHOTOGRAPHERS

Amberg, Gunda 55
Hackenberg, Rainer 12, 19, 22, 24L, 24R, 28, 30, 32, 38, 41, 42, 43, 50, 51, 54, 56, 57, 60, 78, 82, 83, 85
Liese, Knut 8, 13, 16, 25, 26, 49, 62, 64, 66, 67, 70, 72, 73, 75, 76, 80, 81, 84, cover
Reimer, Michael 68, 79
Simon, Gerd 18
Stankiewicz, Thomas 48
Storck, Manfred 3, 36, 37
Taschner, Wolfgang 10, 14, 33, 39, 46
Thiele, Klaus 9, 23, 44

GLOSSARY

English	Spanish	Balearic-Catalan
Good morning / day	*Buenos días*	Bon dia
Good day (after noon)	*Buenas tardes*	Bona tarda
Good night	*Buenas noches*	Bona nit
Hello (among friends)	*¡Hola!*	Hola! Uèp!
Goodbye	*Adiós*	Adéu
See you	*Hasta la vista*	A reveure
Til tomorrow	*Hasta mañana*	Fins demà.
How are you?	*¿Qué tal?*	Com anam?
Thanks!	*Gracias*	Gràcies
Please (request)	*Por favor*	Per favor, sisplau
Excuse me	*Perdón*	Perdó
I'm sorry	*Lo siento*	Me sap greu
Yes / no	*Si / No*	Si / No
A little slower please	*Mas lento, por favor*	Més a poc a poc, per favor
What is your name?	*¿Cómo se llama Usted?*	Com et dius?
My name is ...	*Me llamo ...*	Me diuen ...
How do I get to ...?	*¿Cómo llego a ...?*	Com s'hi va a ...?
Where can I find ...?	*¿Donde hay ...?*	On puc trobar ...?
Where are the toilets?	*¿Donde hay los baños?*	On són es lavabos?
Who / when / where to?	*¿Quien / Cuando / Adonde?*	Qui / Quan / Cap a on?
What?	*¿Qué?*	Què?
How much does ... cost?	*¿Cuanto cuesta ...?*	Quant costa ...?
How much is that?	*¿Cuanto es?*	Quant fa?
How far is it to ...?	*¿Cuantos kilómetros son hasta ...?*	Com és de lluny ...?
What time is it?	*¿Qué hora es?*	Quina hora és?
Yesterday / today / tomorrow	*ayer / hoy / mañana*	ahir / avui / demà
Very well / not well	*muy bien / mal*	molt bo / mal
expensive / cheap	*caro / barrato*	car(a) / barat(a)
To the left / right	*A la izquierda / derecha*	a l'esquerra / a la dreta
Above / below	*arriba / abajo*	dalt / a baix
Straight ahead	*Siempre derecho*	recte
Car / taxi	*coche / taxi*	cotxe / taxi
Boat / harbor	*barco / puerto*	vaixell / port
Ticket	*billete*	bitllett
There (and back)	*ida (y vuelta)*	anada (i tornada)
Bon appetit!	*¡Que aproveche!*	Bon profit!
The bill please!	*¡La cuenta, por favor!*	Es compte, sisplau!
Open / closed	*abierto / cerrado*	obert / tancat
Post office / stamp	*Correos / sello*	Correus / segell
0 / 1 / 2	*cero / un(o) / dos*	zero / u (un, una) / dues
3 / 4 / 5	*tres / cuatro / cinco*	tres / quatre / cinc
6 / 7 / 8	*seis / siete / ocho*	sis / set / vuit
9 / 10 / 11 / 12	*nueve / diez / once / doce*	nou / deu / onze / dotze
20 / 50 / 100	*veinte / cincuenta / cien(to)*	vint / cinquanta / cent
1,000 / 10,000	*mil / diez mil*	mil / deu mil